IN THE DELICATF

ELEGANCE OF AN

ORCHID, FIND

INSPIRATION FOR

YOUR OUWN GRACEFUL

GROUWTH

CALANTHE

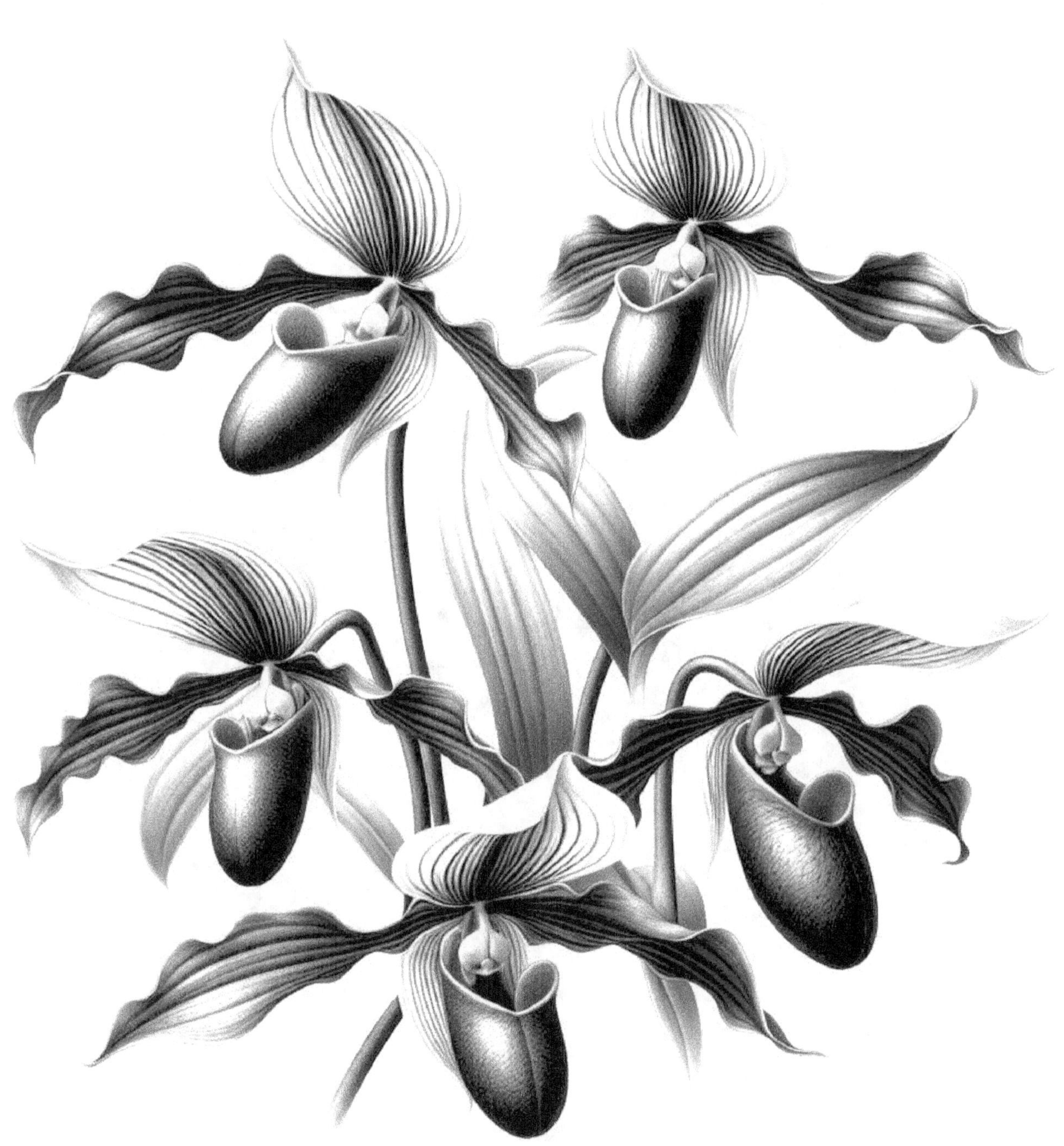

CALANTHE

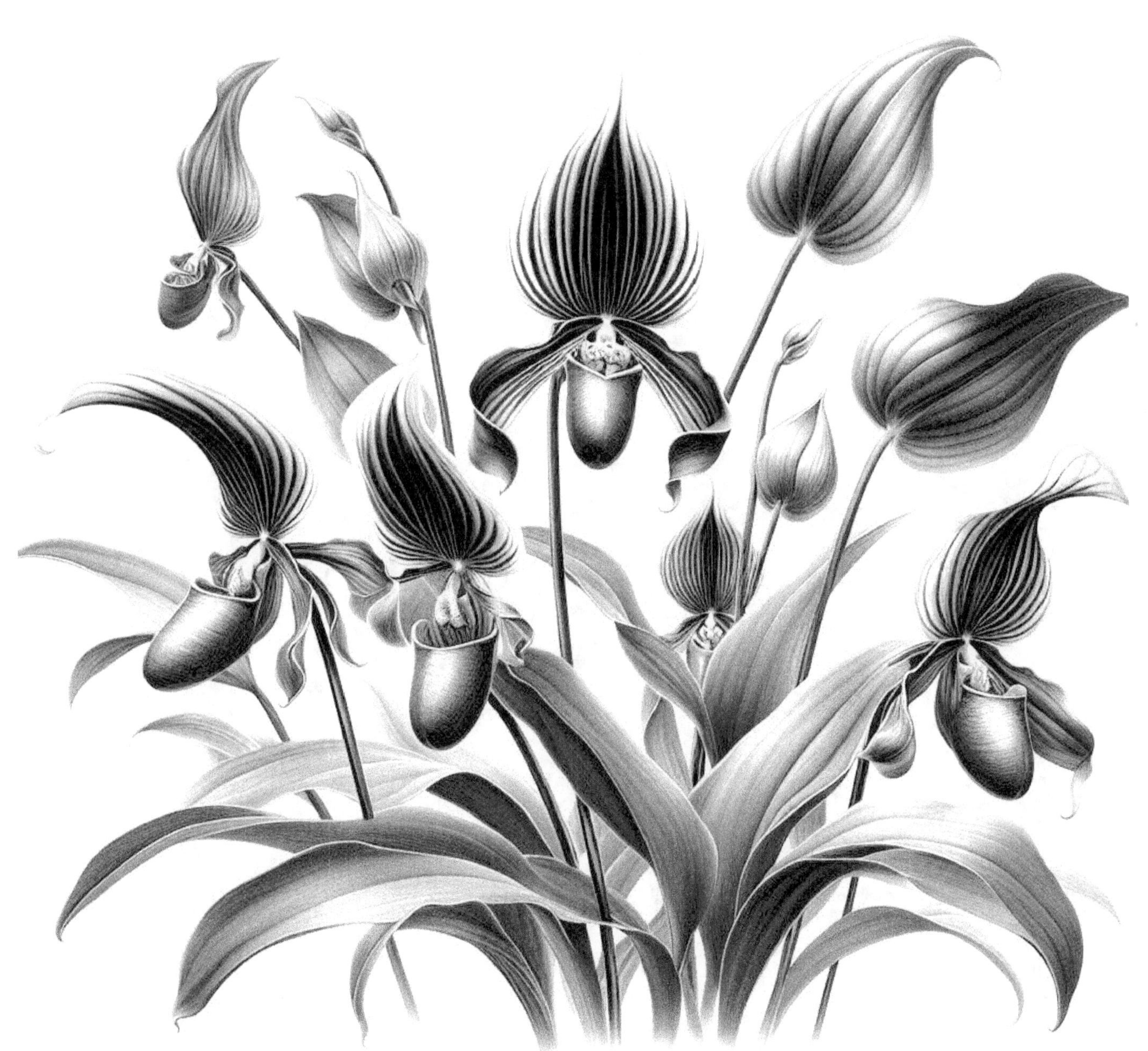

CALANTHE

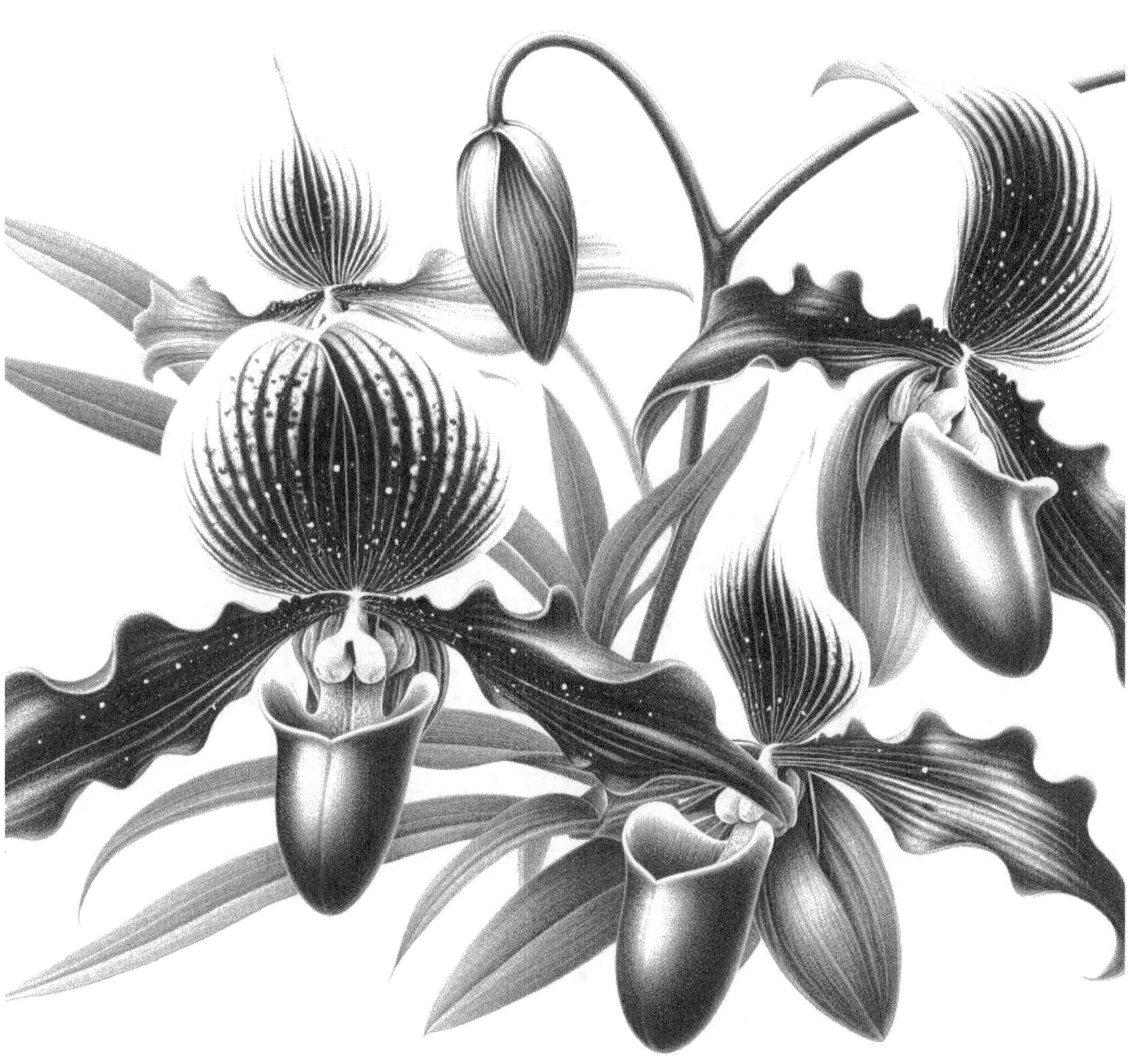

CALANTHE

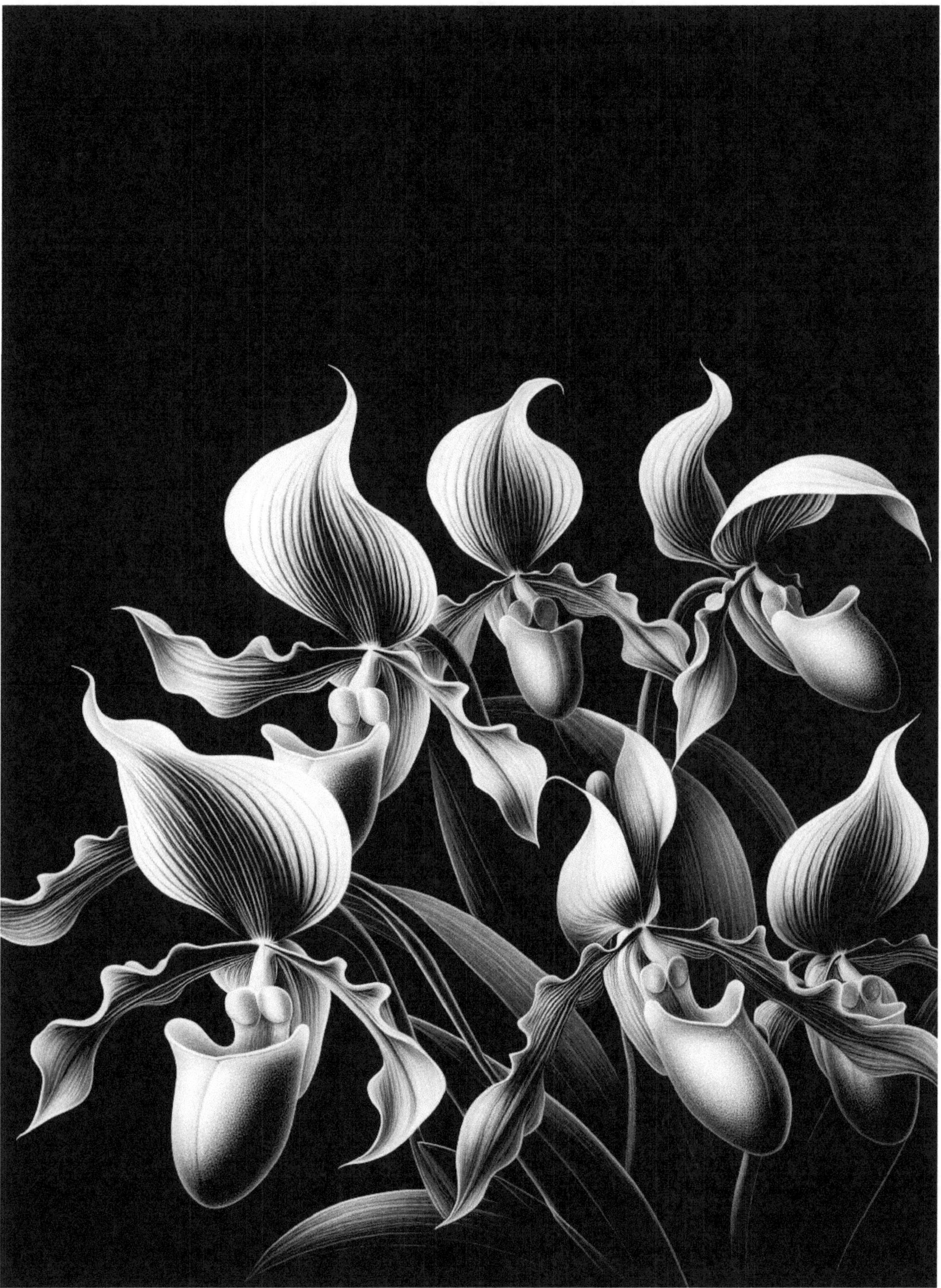

CATTLEYA

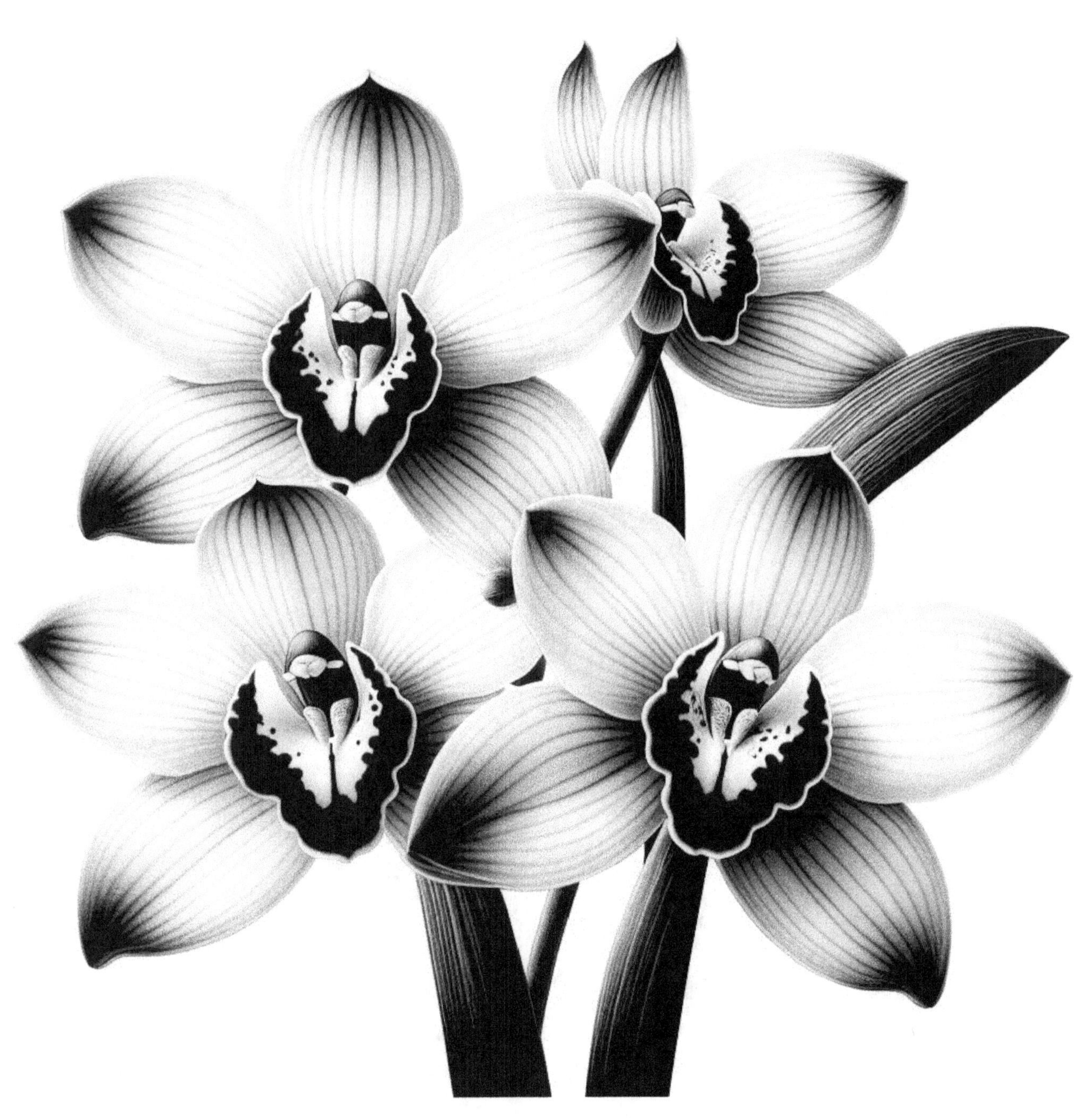

CATTLEYA

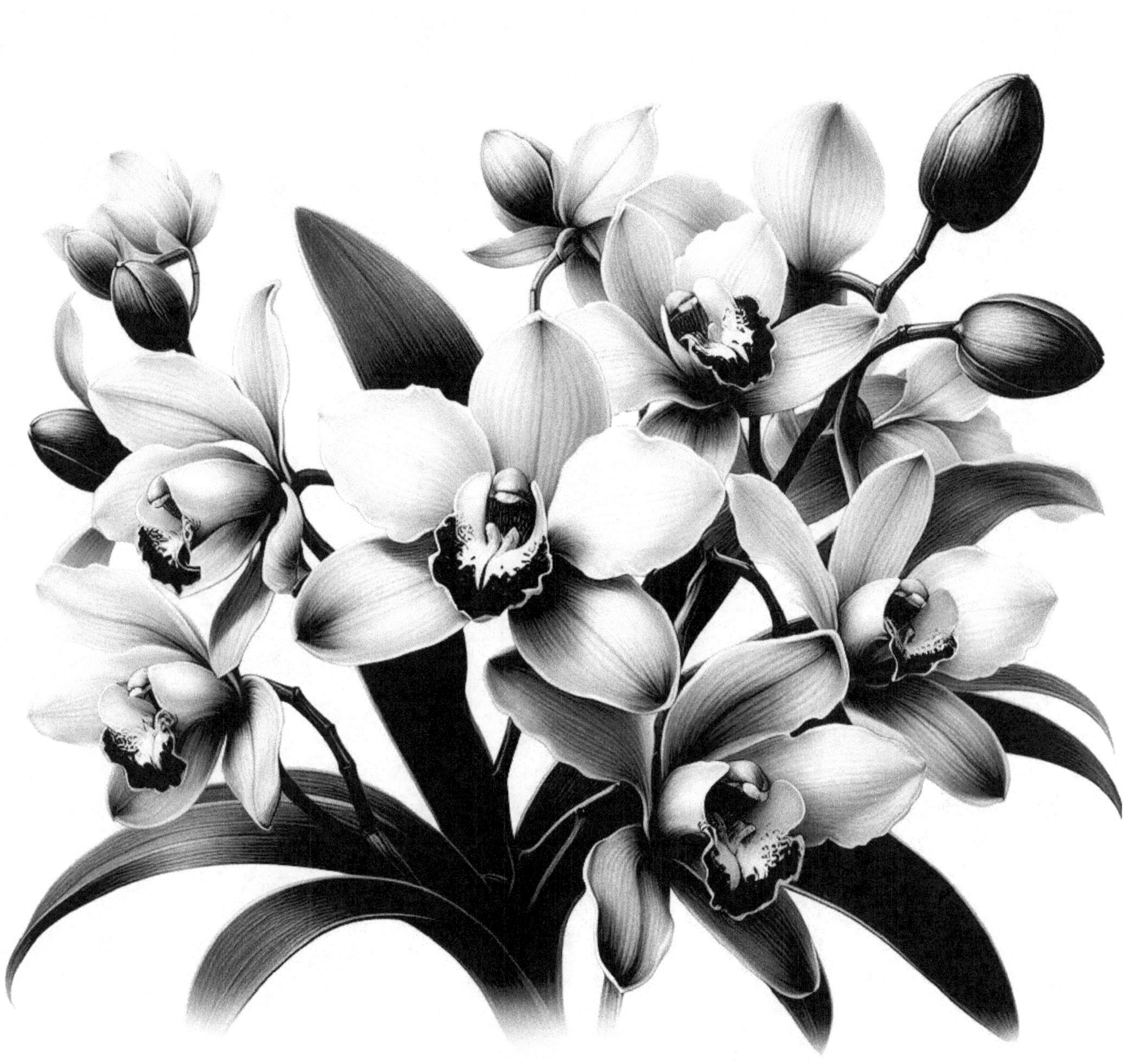

CATTLEYA

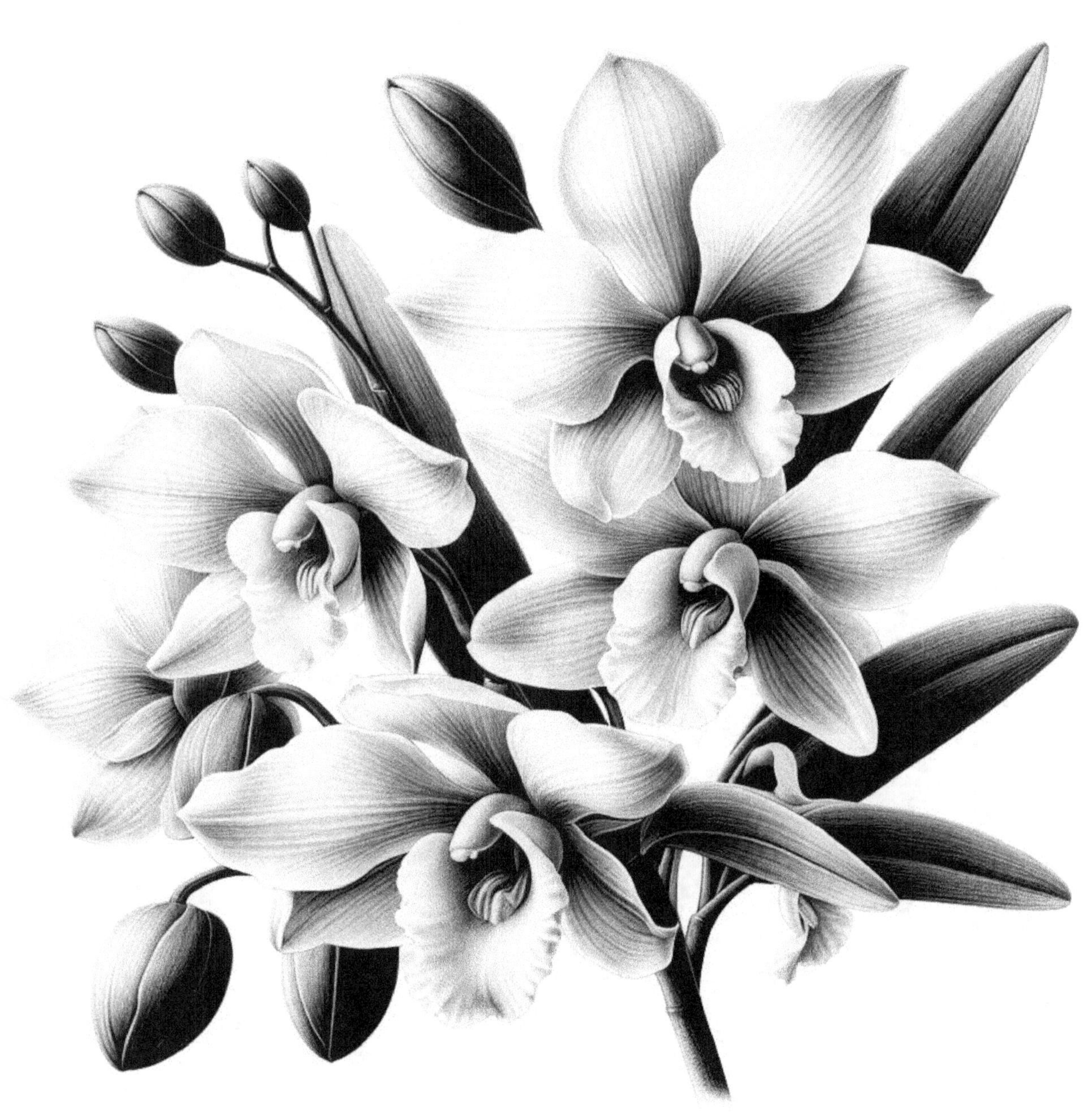

CATTLEYA

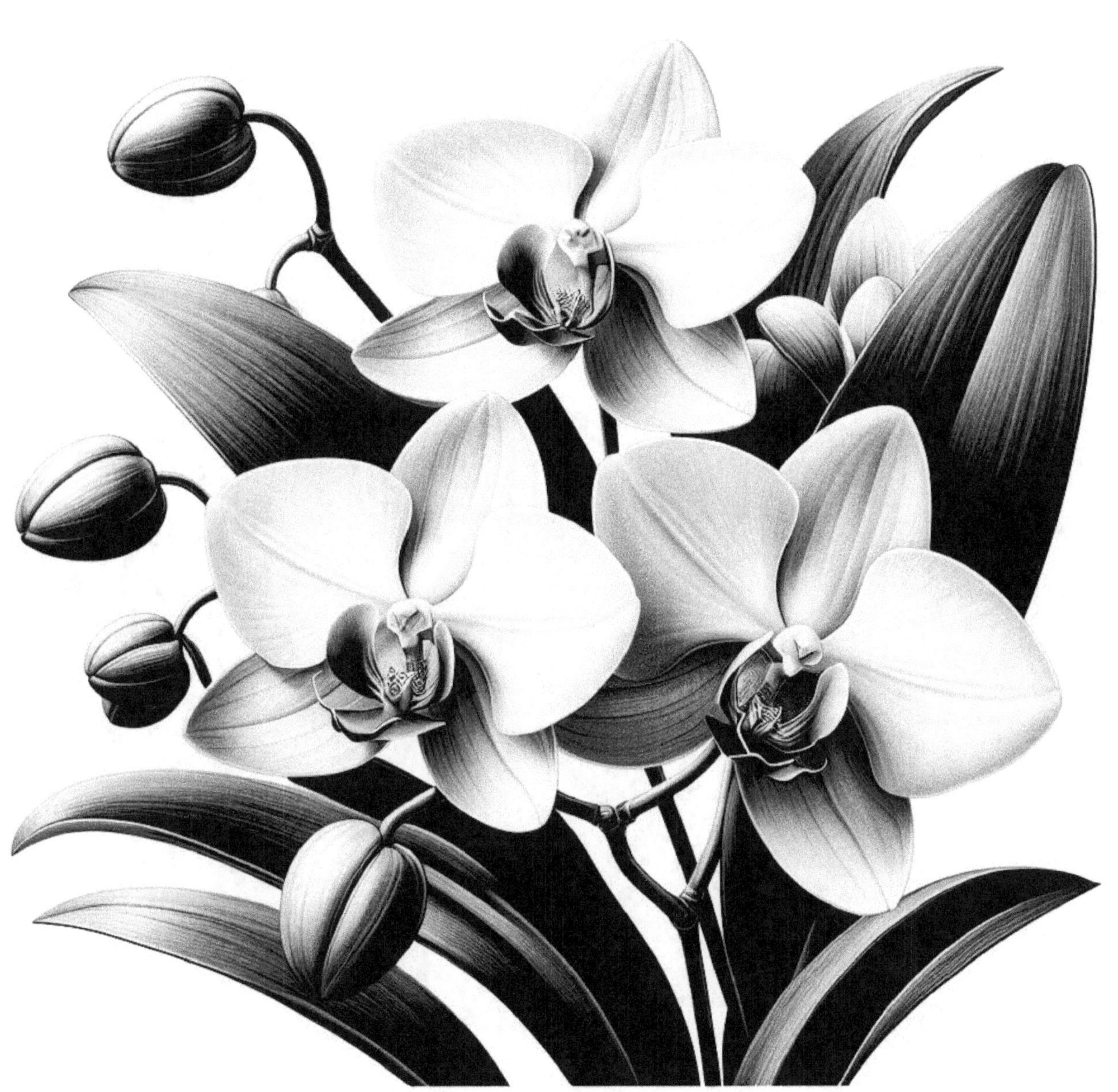

CYMBIDIUM

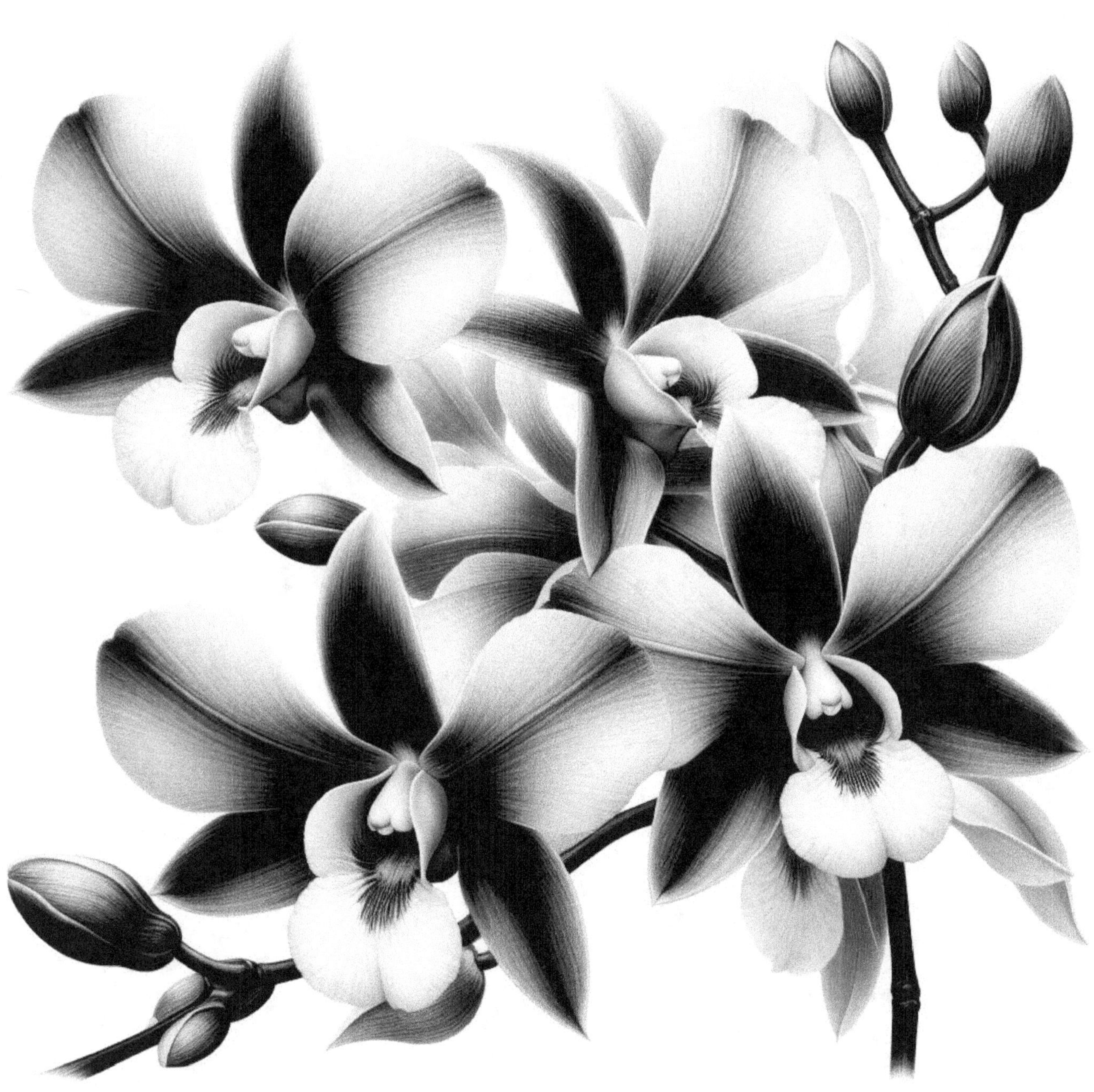

CYMBIDIUM

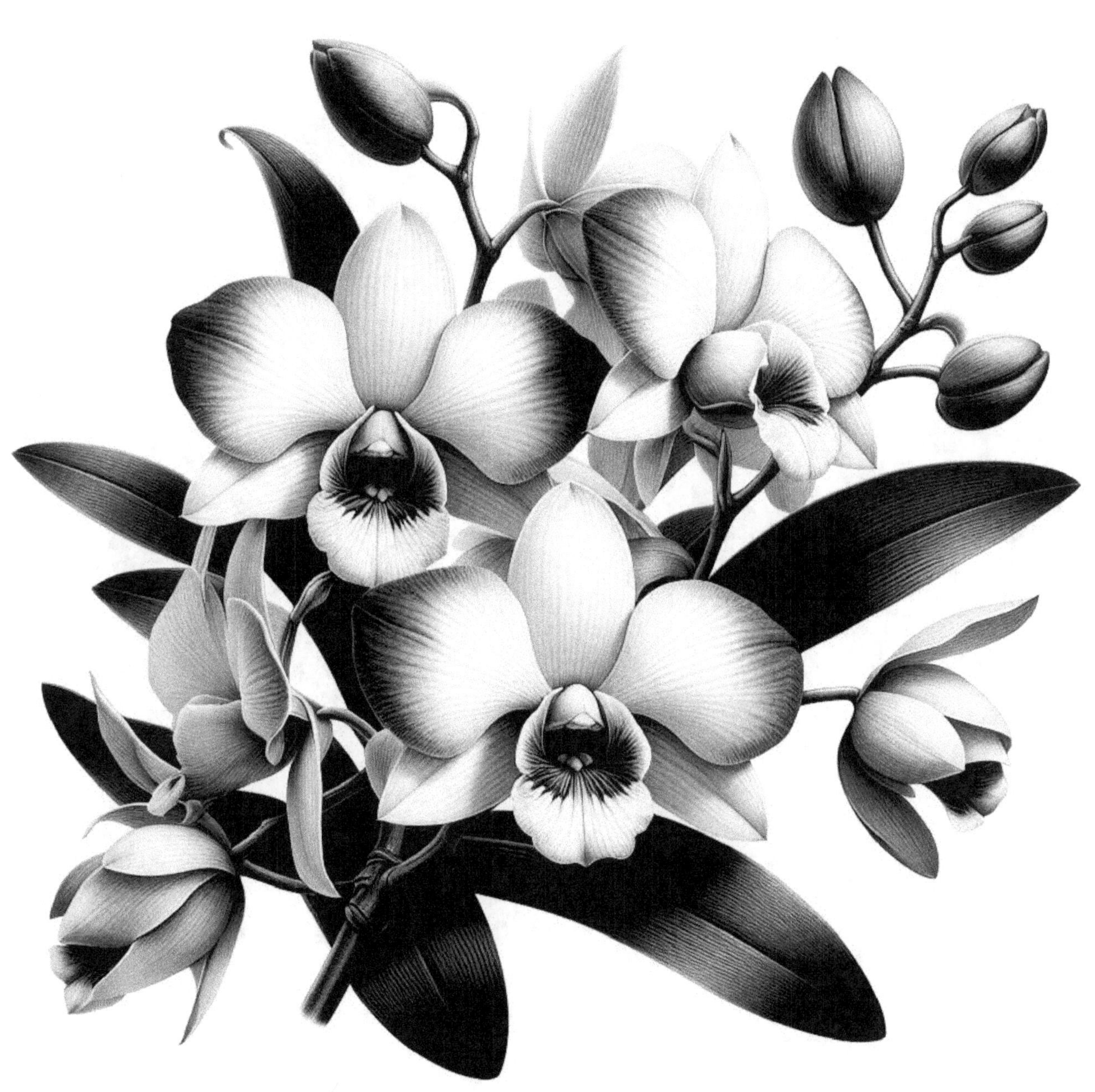

CYMBIDIUM

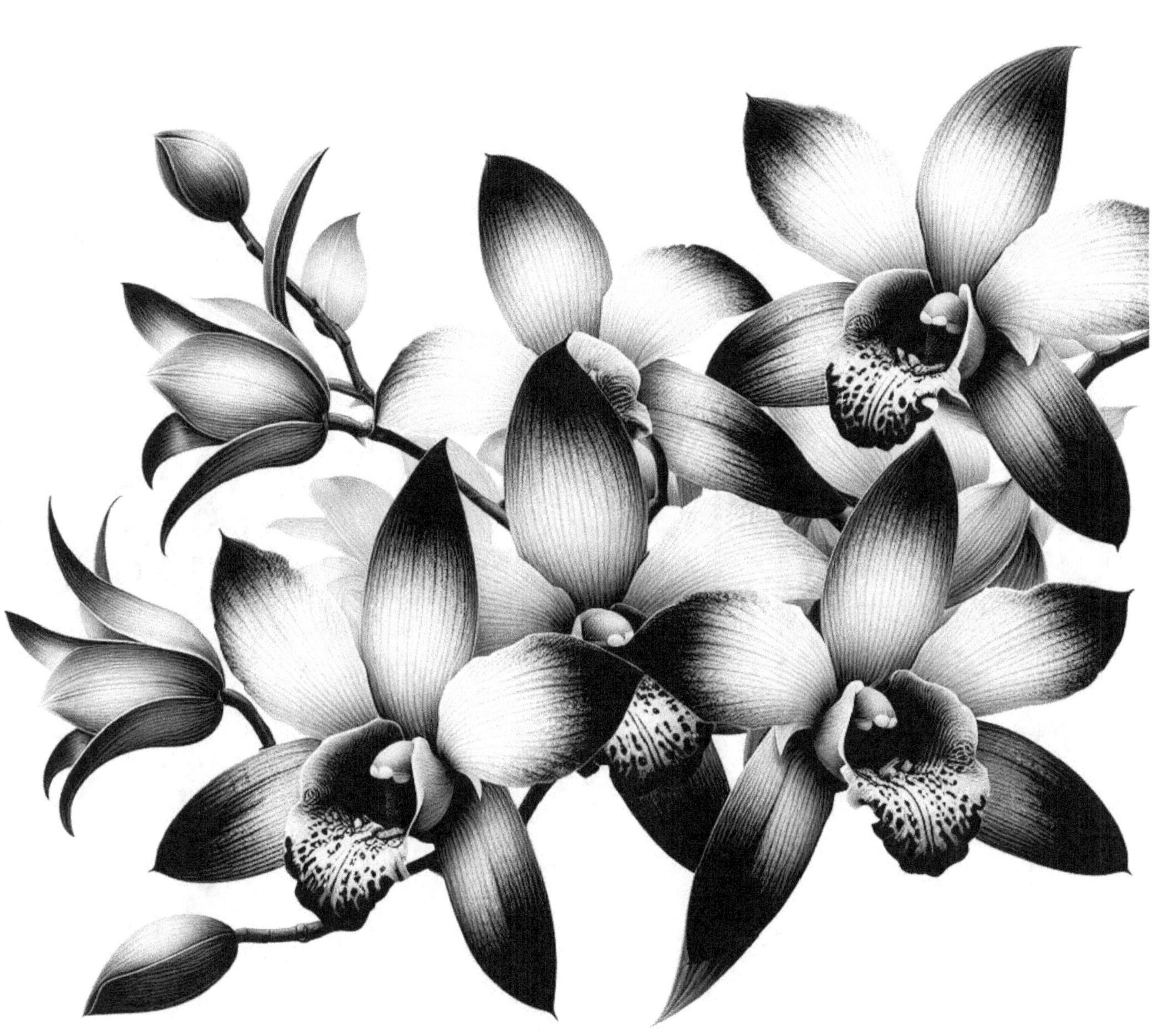

CYMBIDIUM

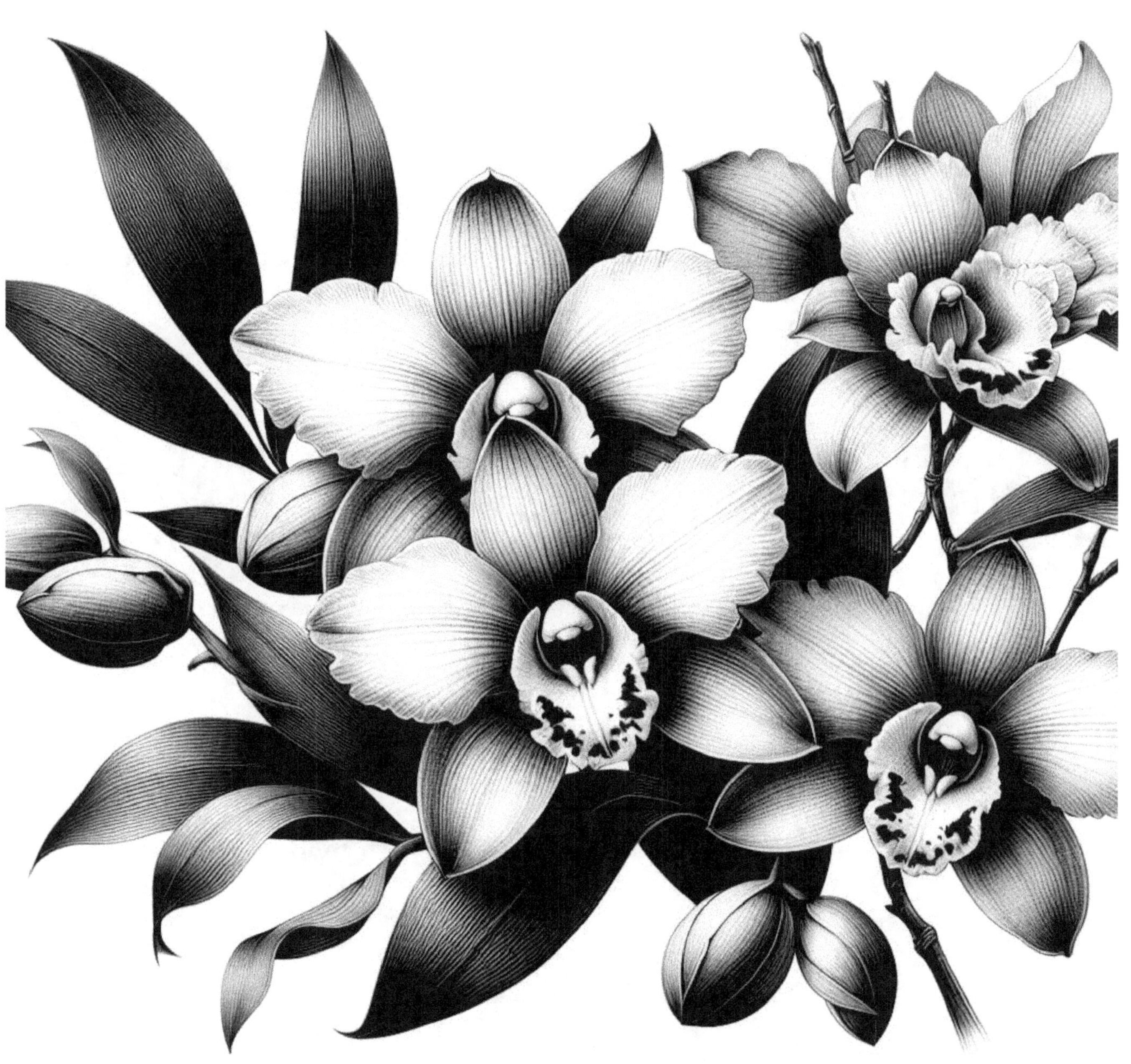

MASDEVALLA

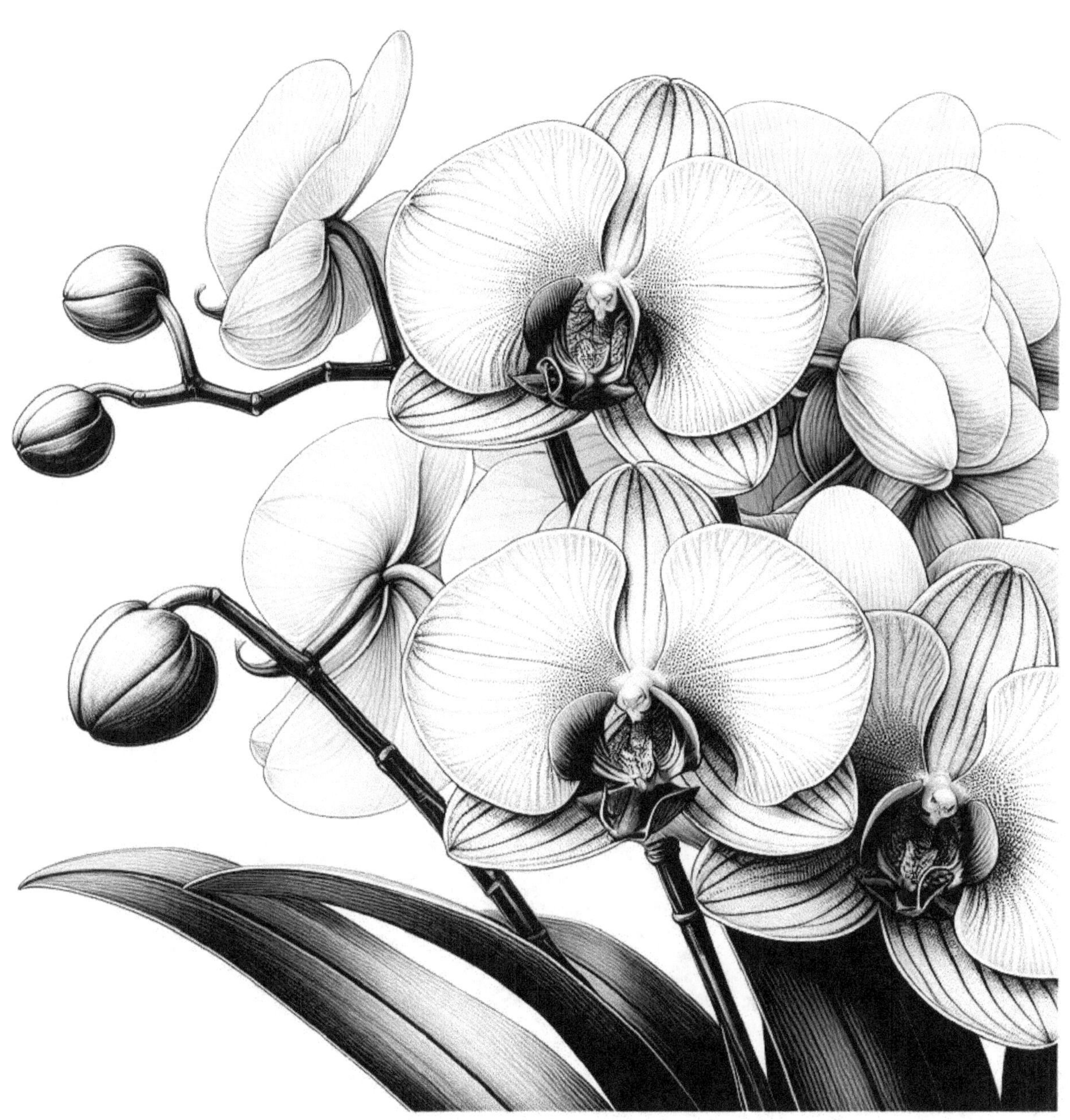

MASDEVALLA

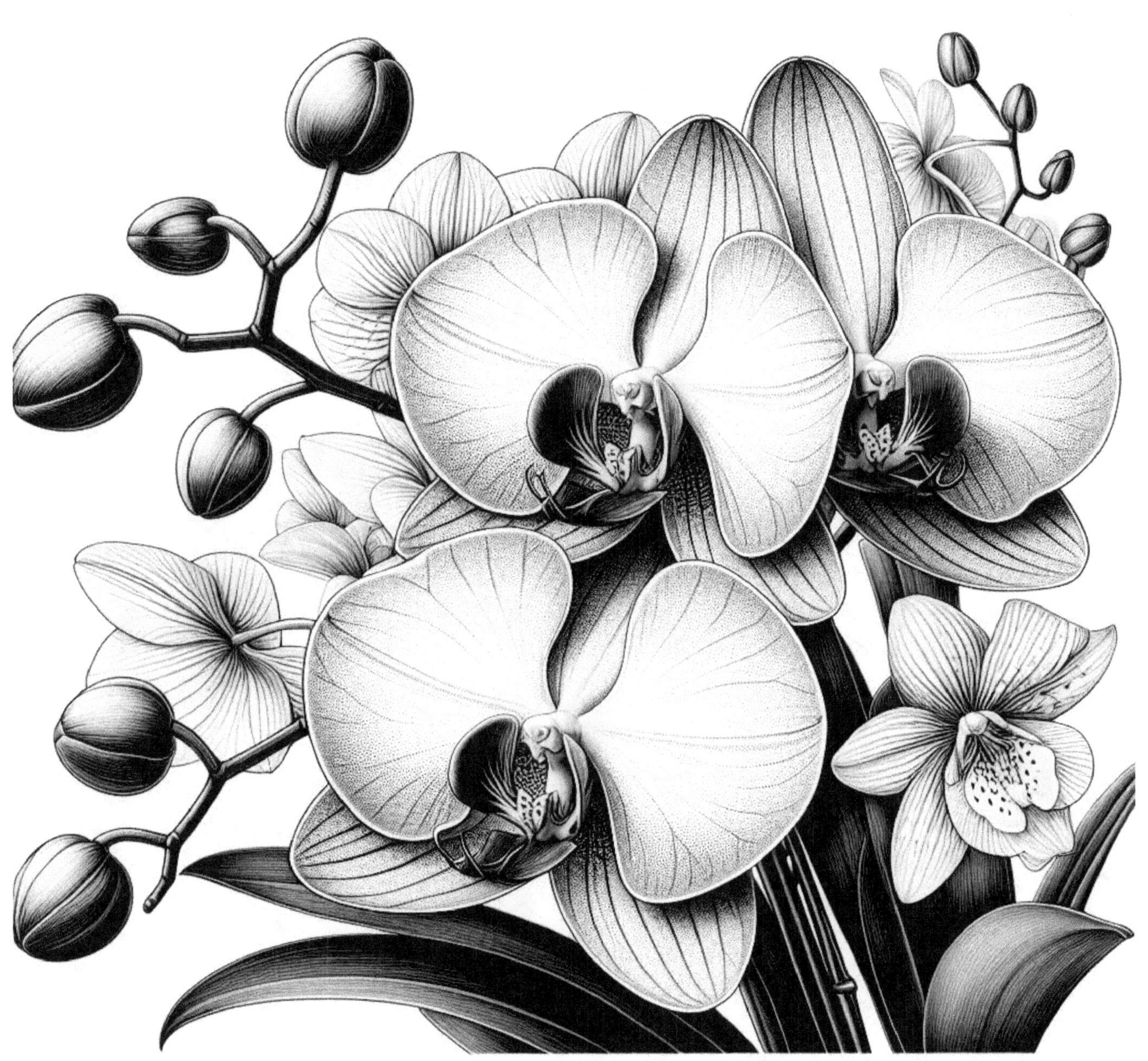

MASDEVALLA

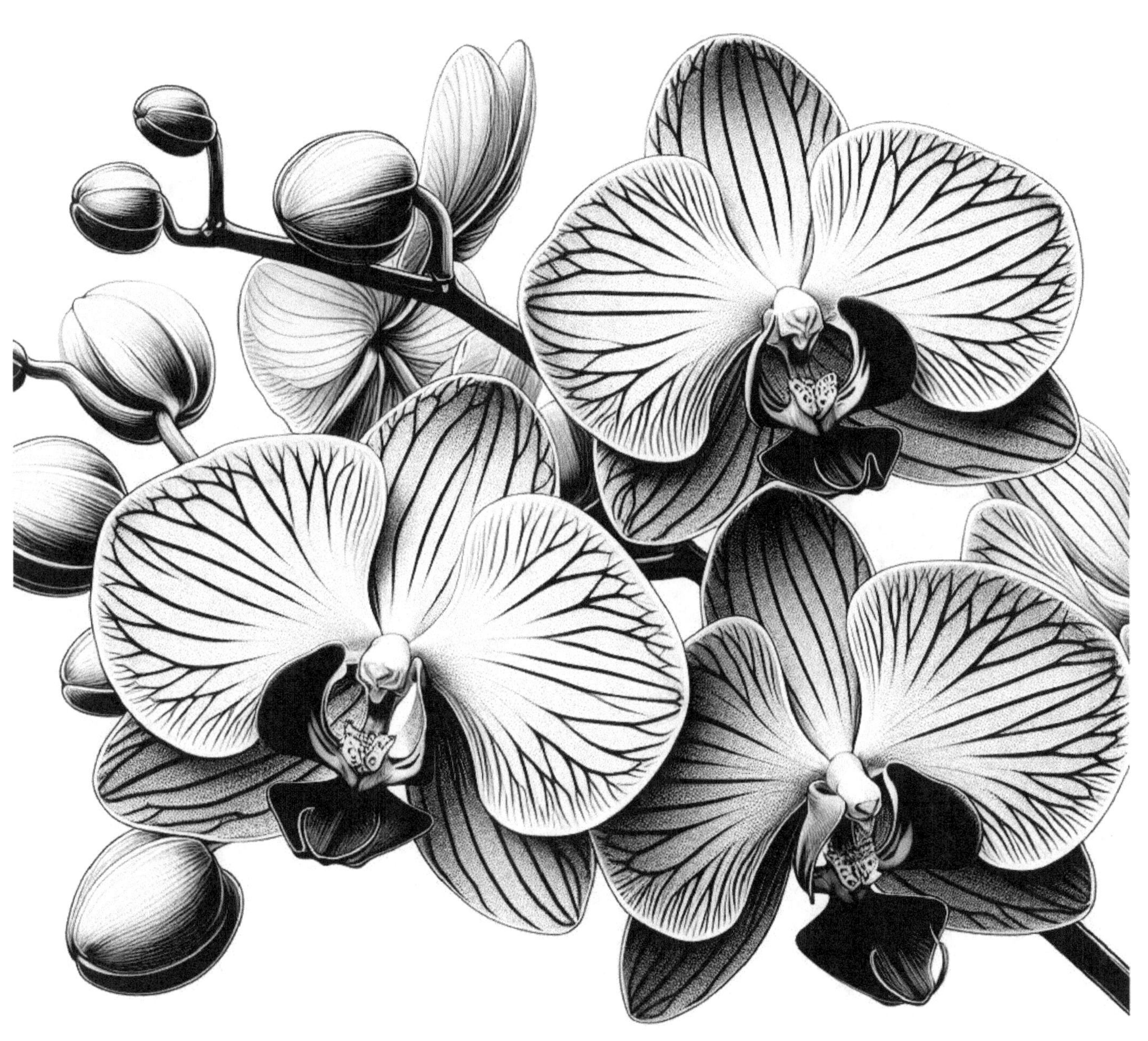

MASDEVALLA

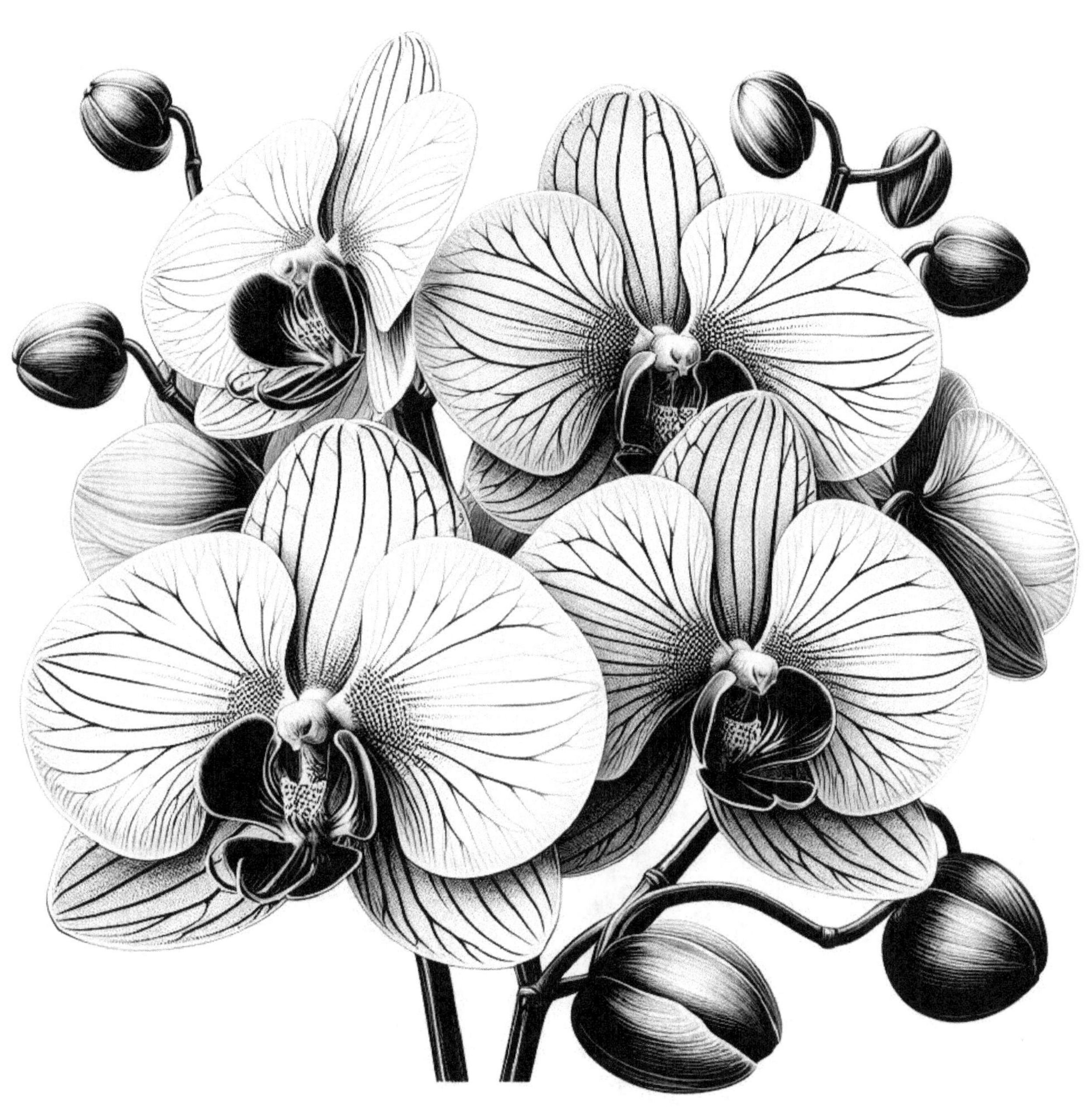

AERANGIS

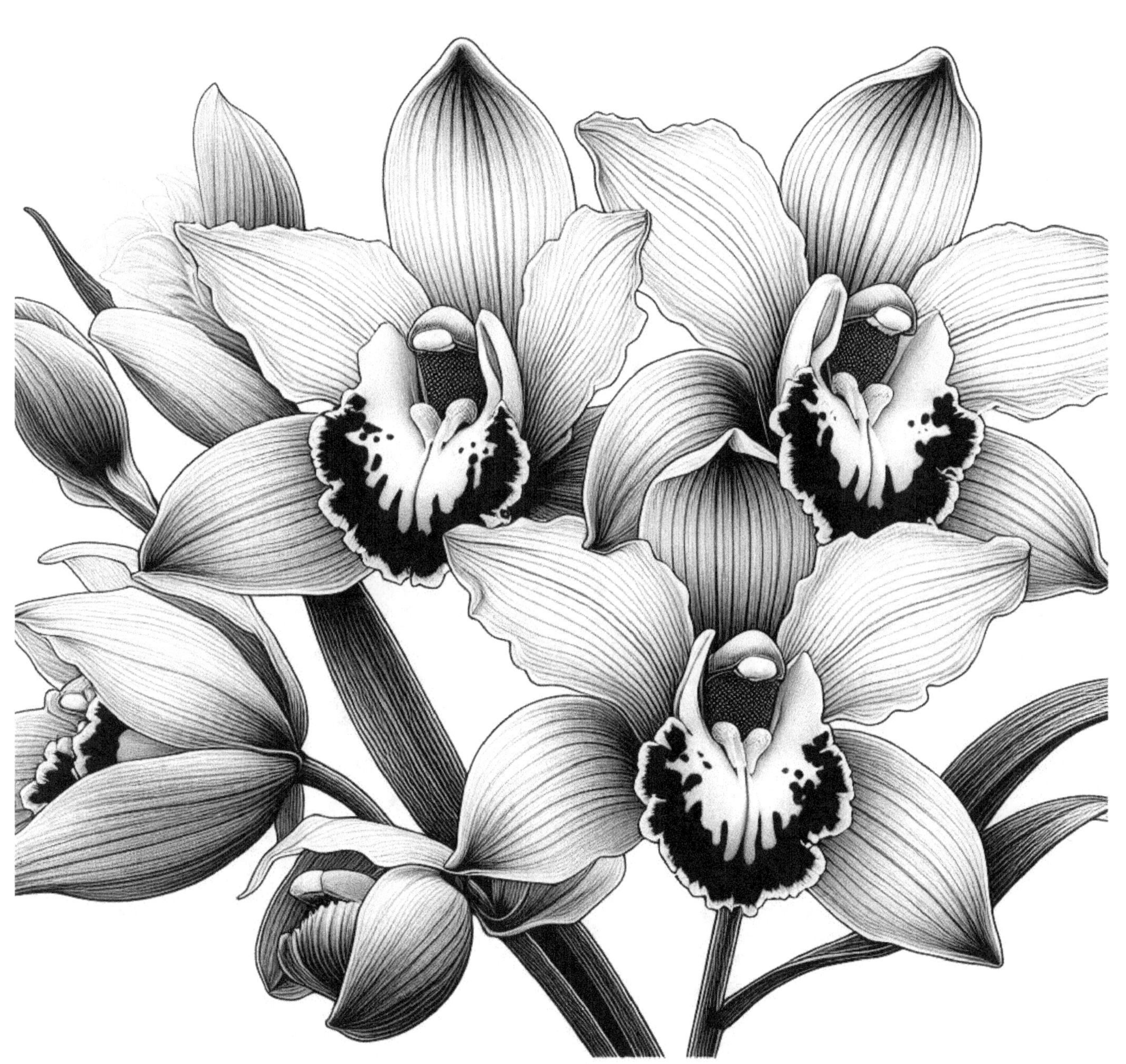

AERANGIS

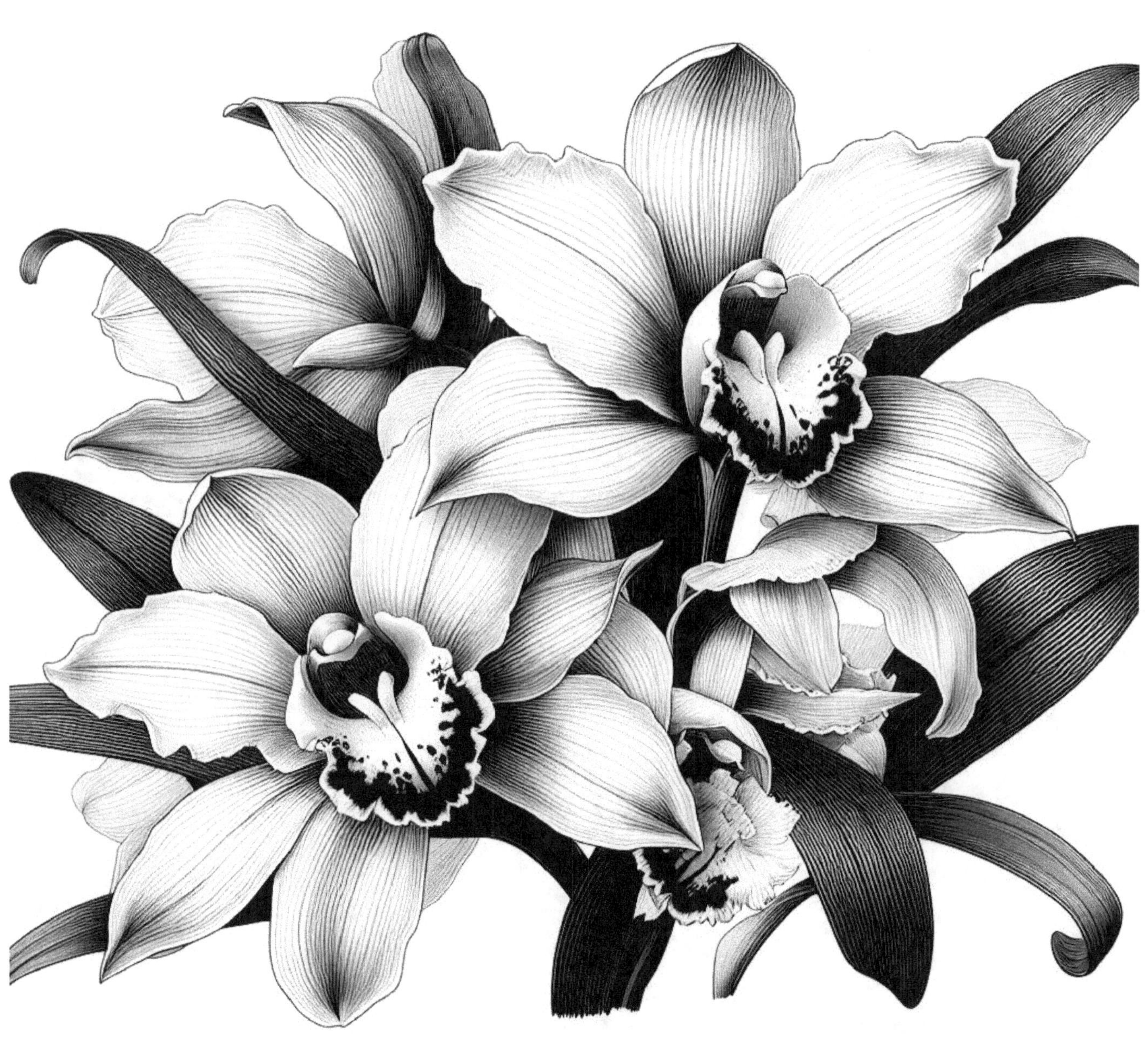

AERANGIS

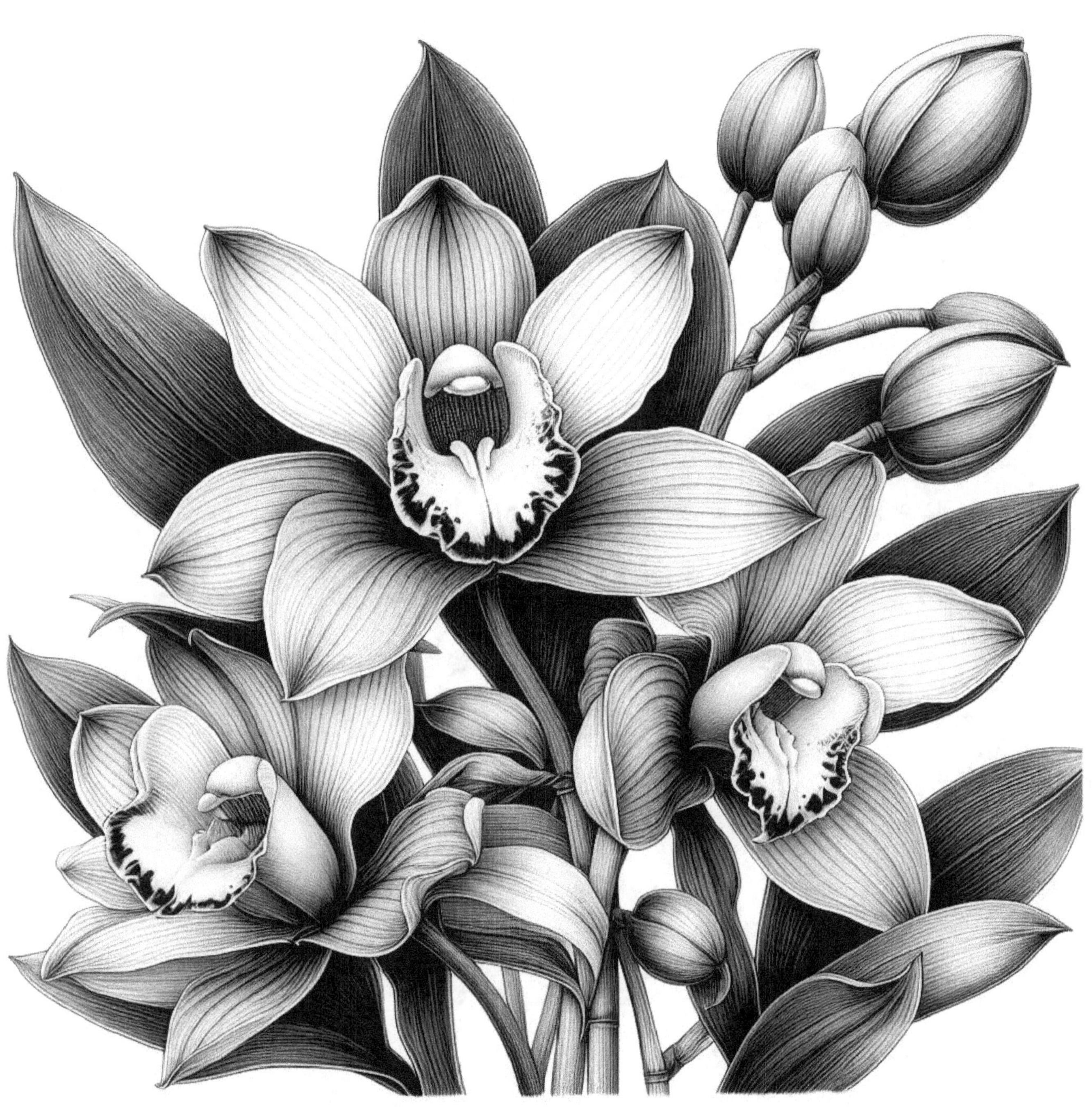

AERANGIS

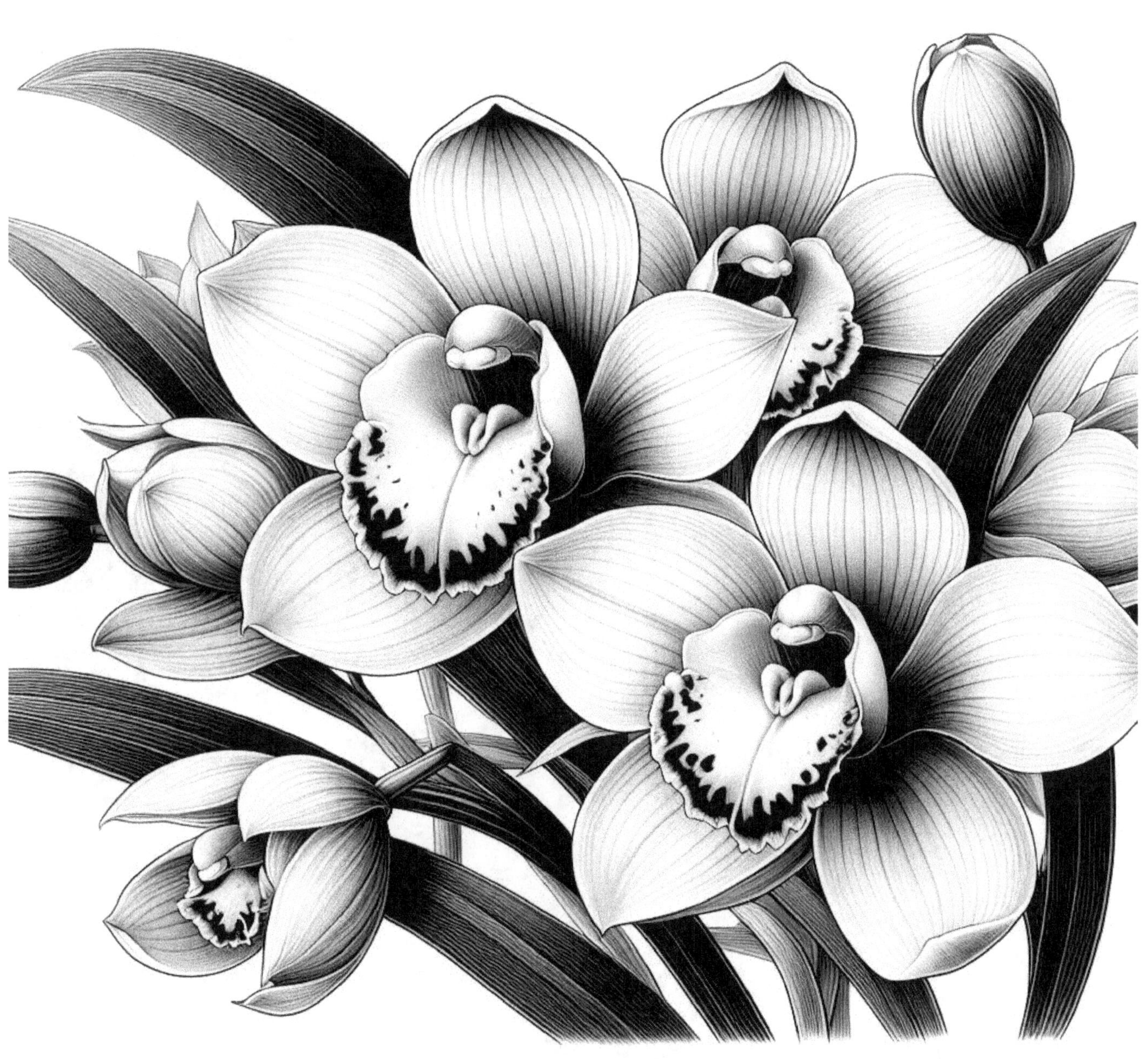

DENDROBIUM

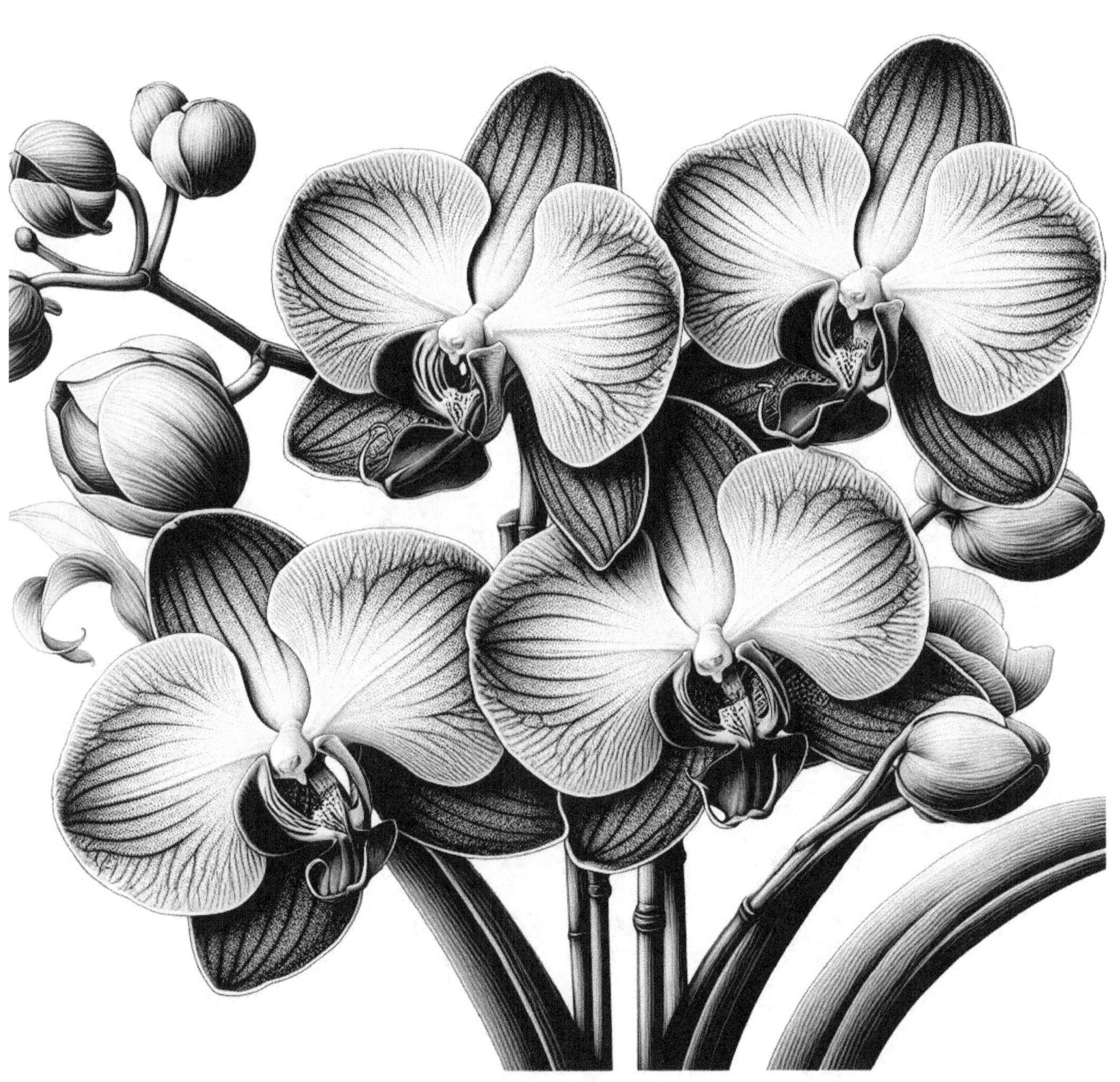

DENDROBIUM

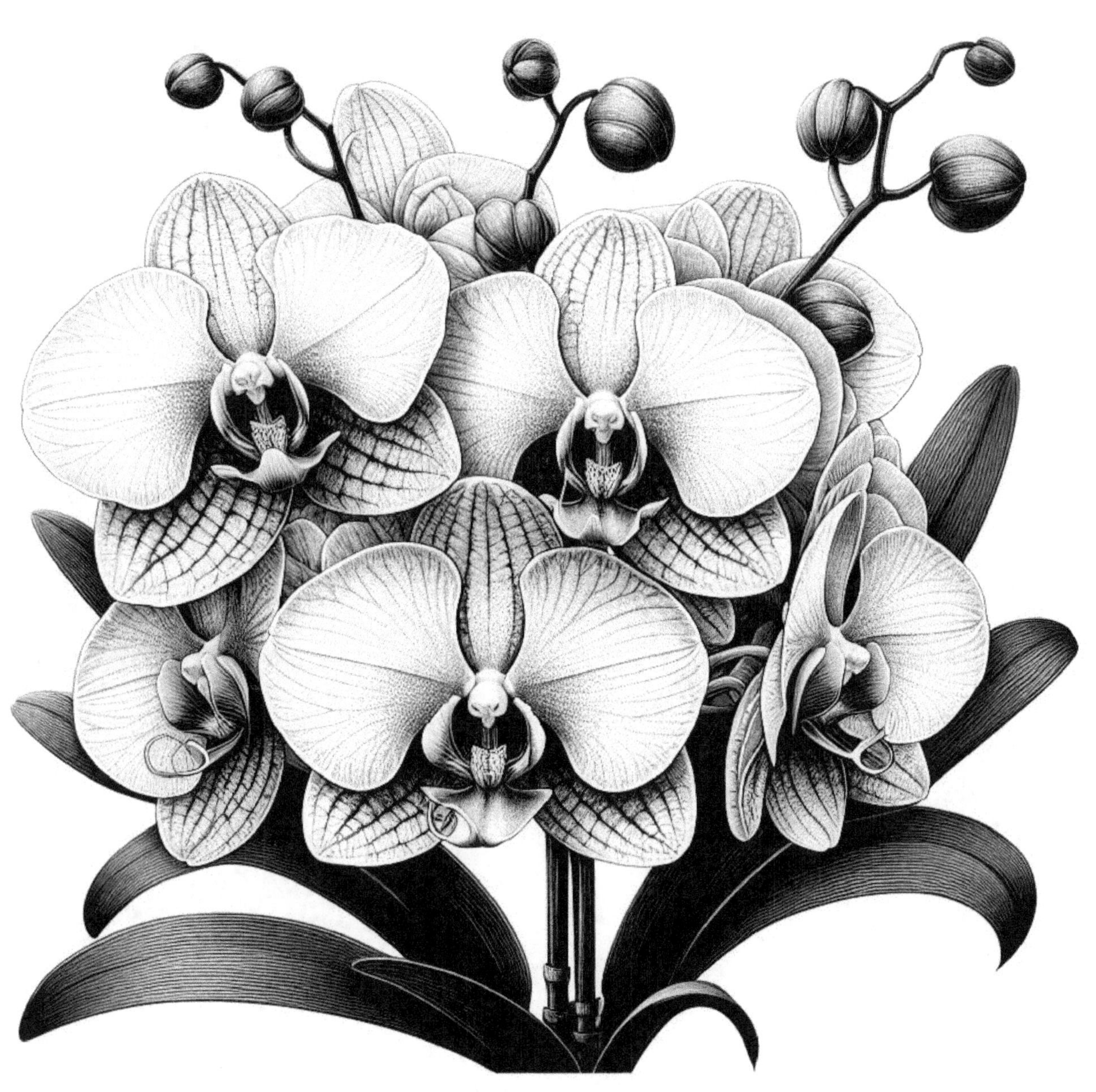

DENDROBIUM

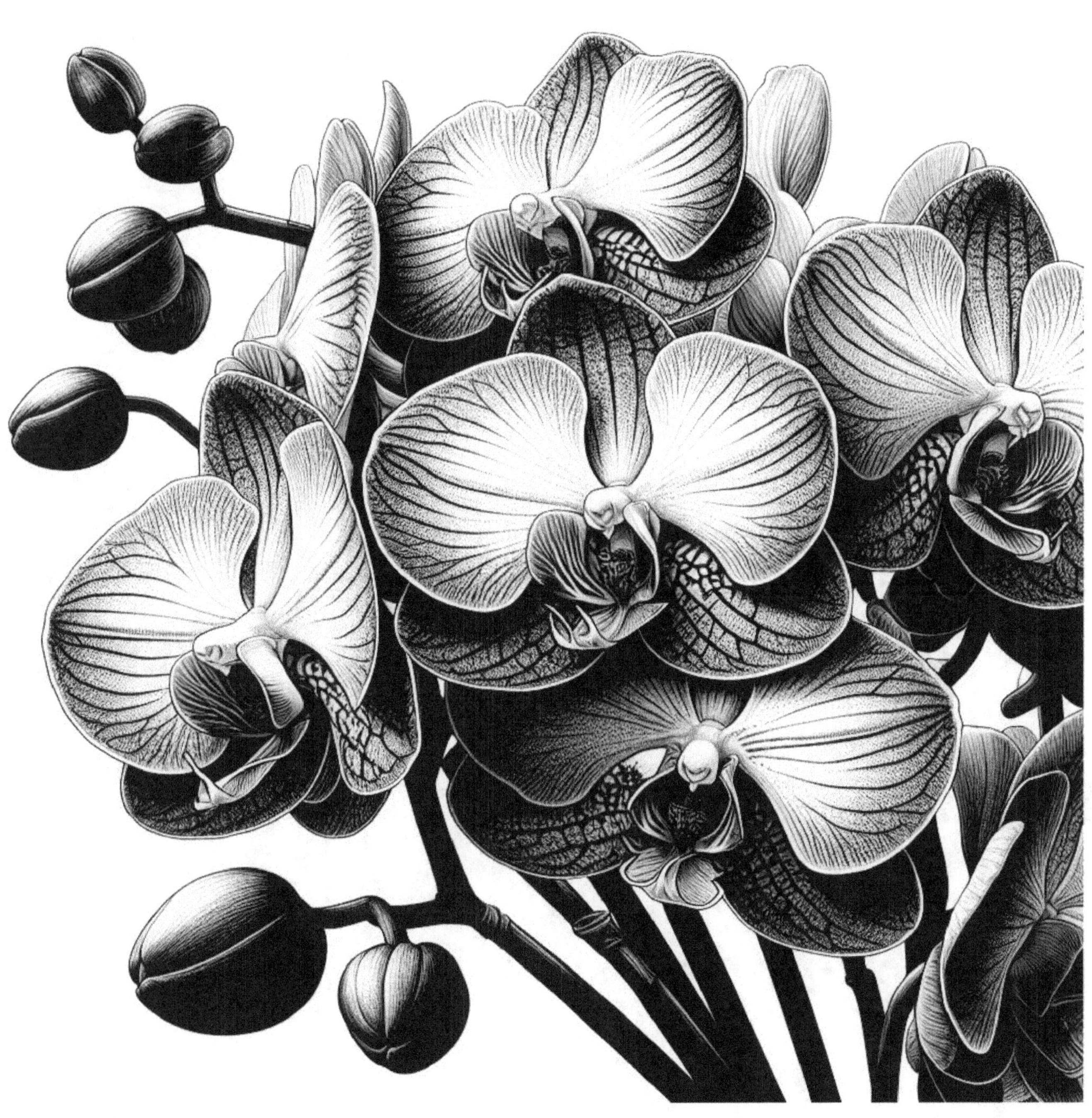

DENDROBIUM

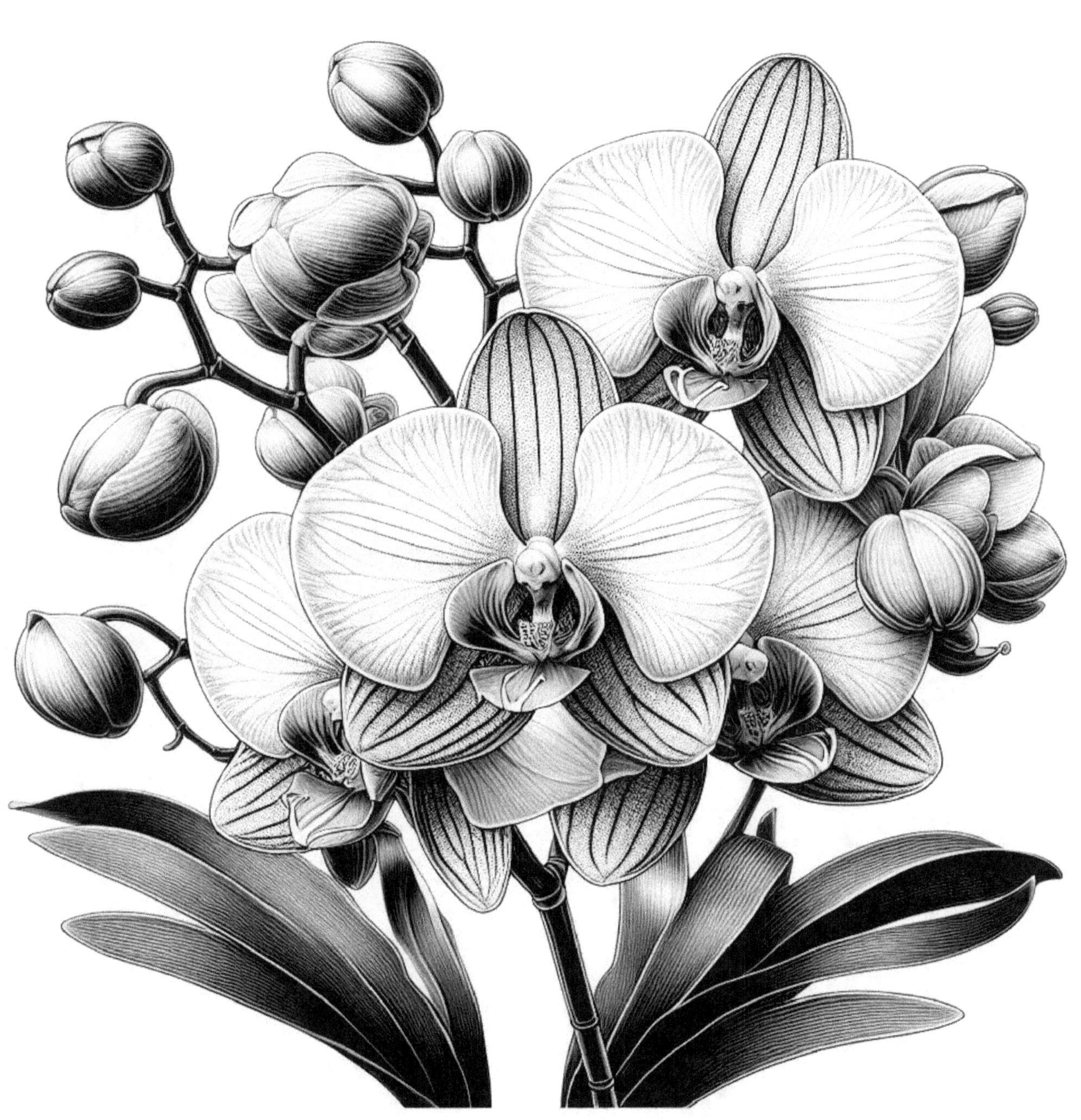

PHALAENOPSIS

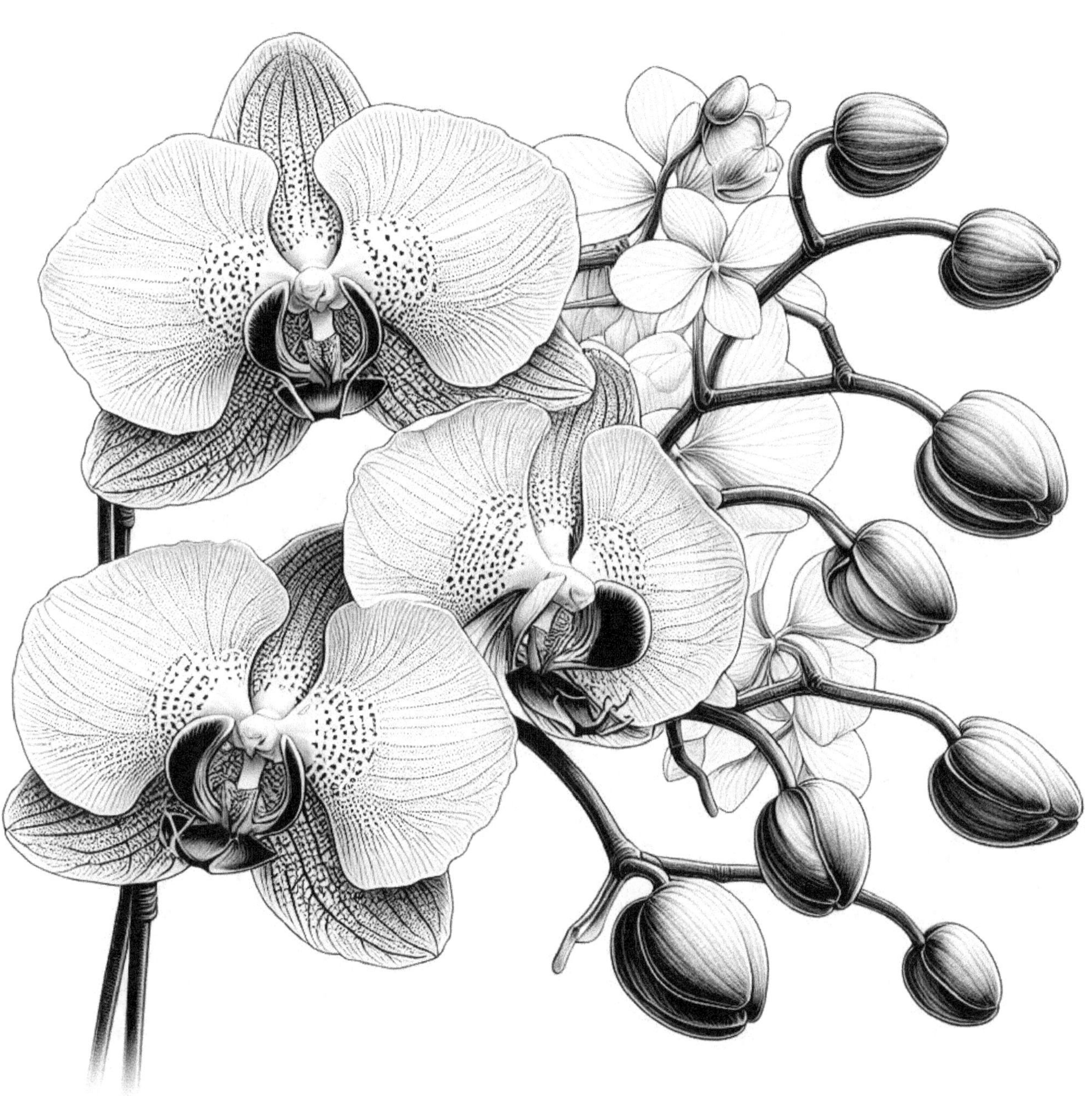

PHALAENOPSIS

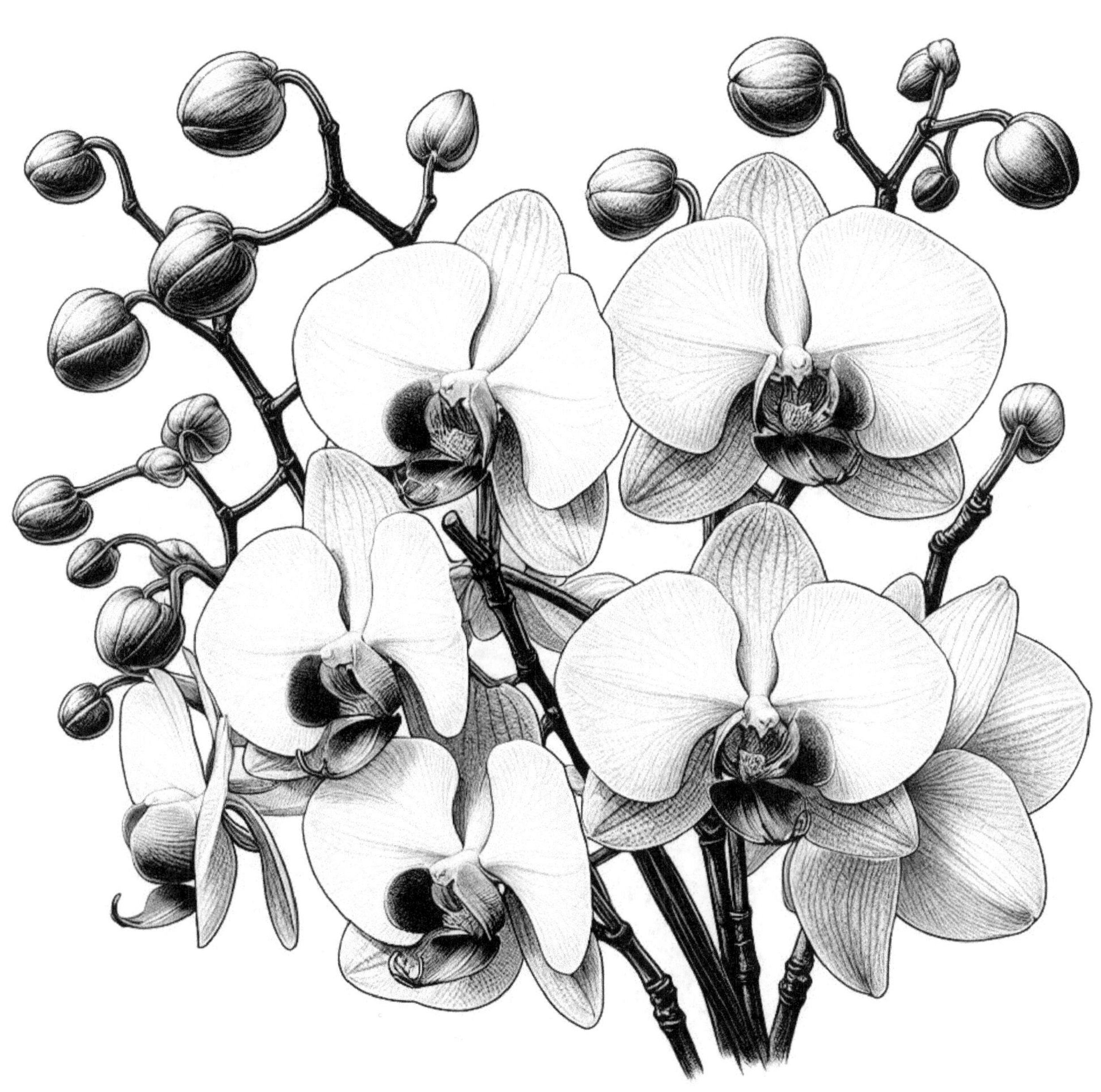

PHALAENOPSIS

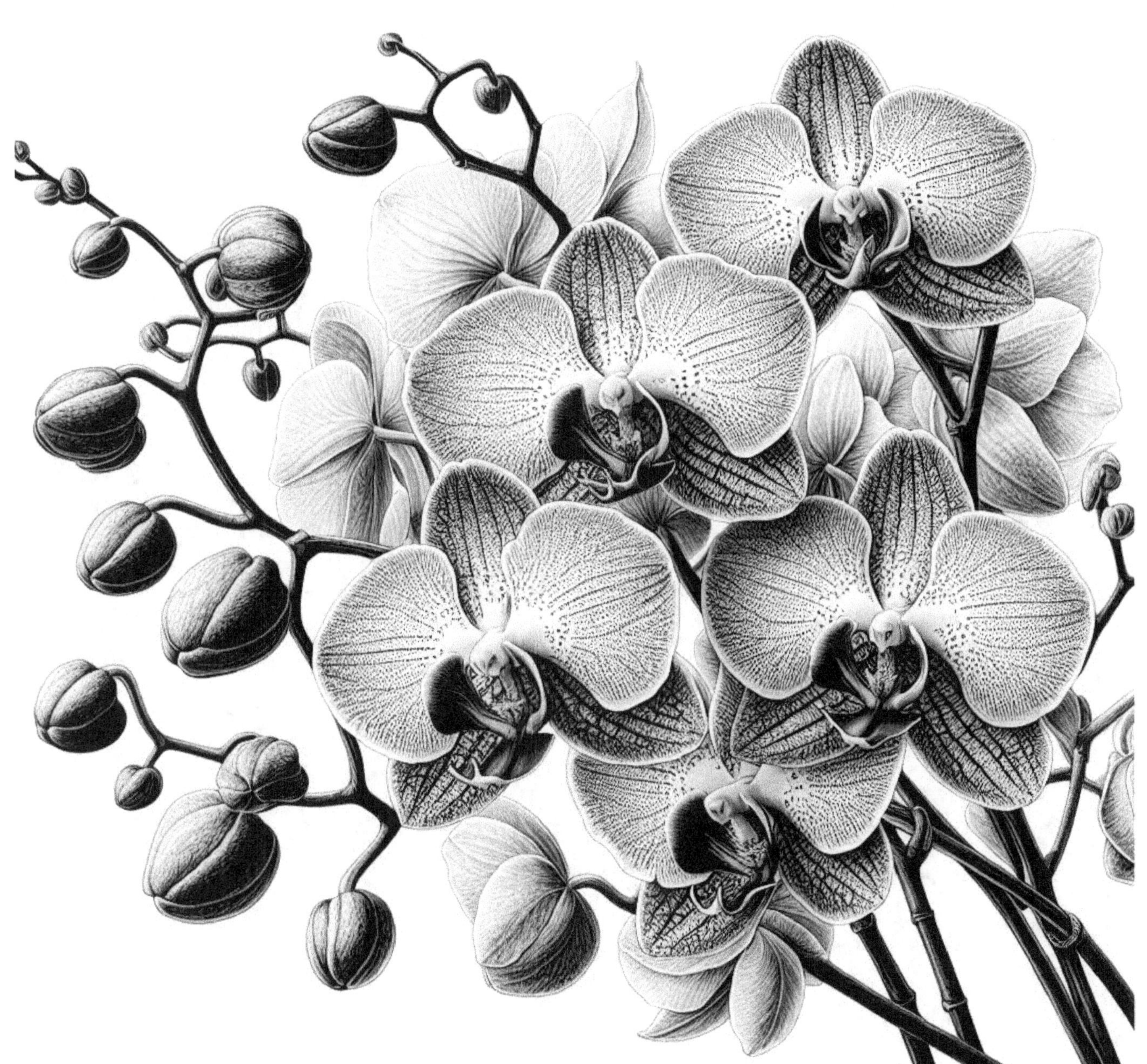

PHALAENOPSIS

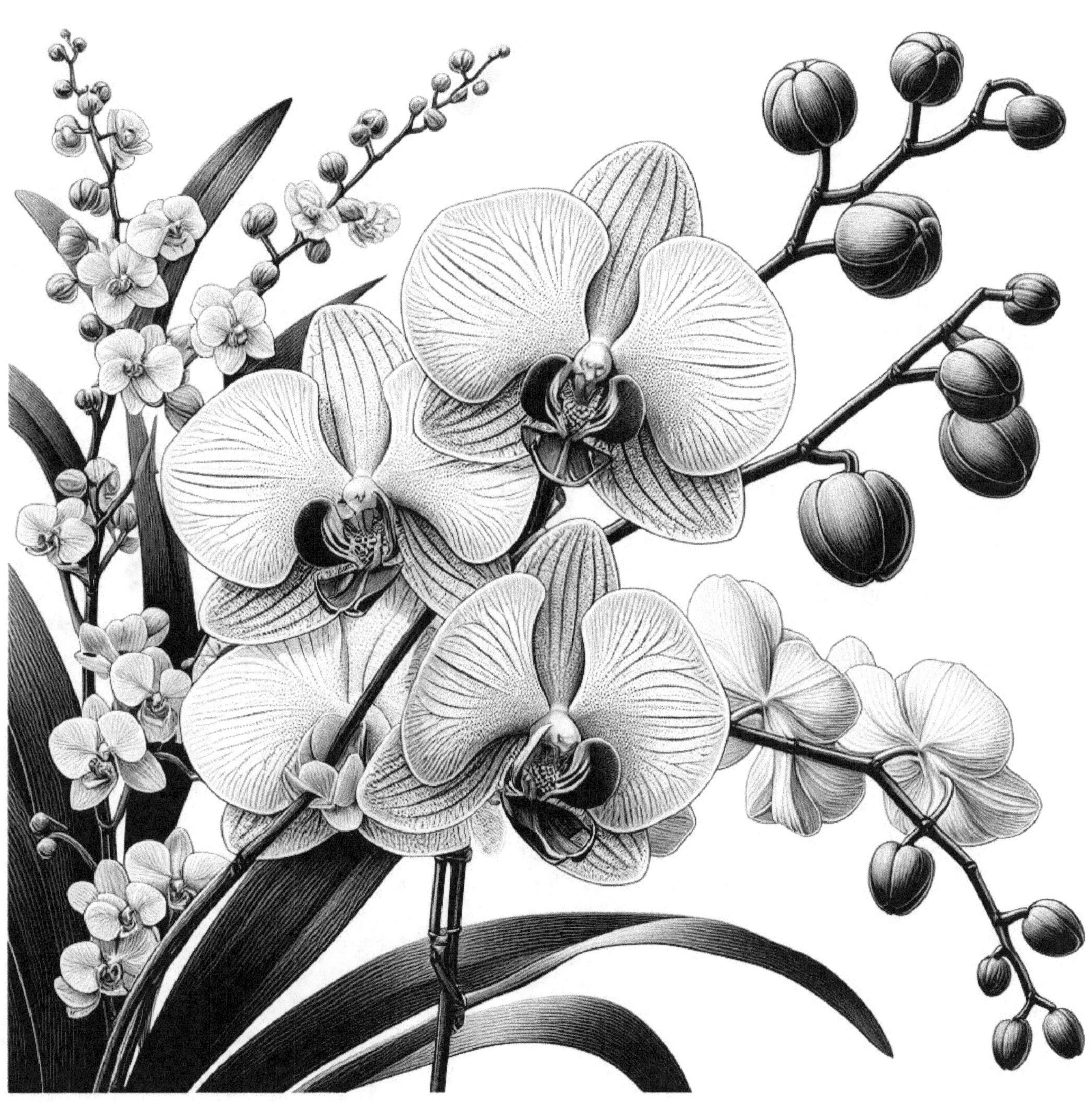

COELOGYNE

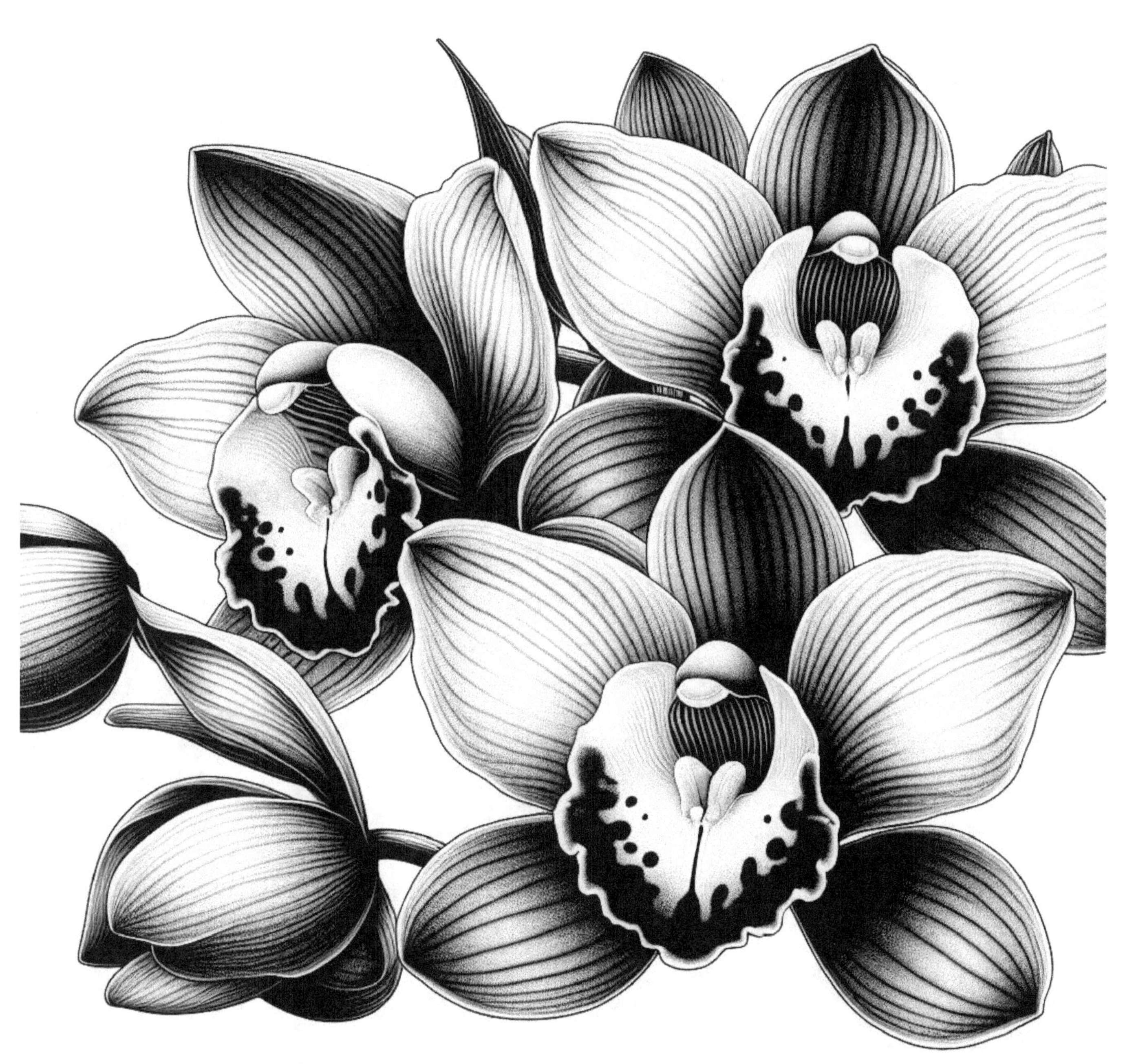

COELOGYNE

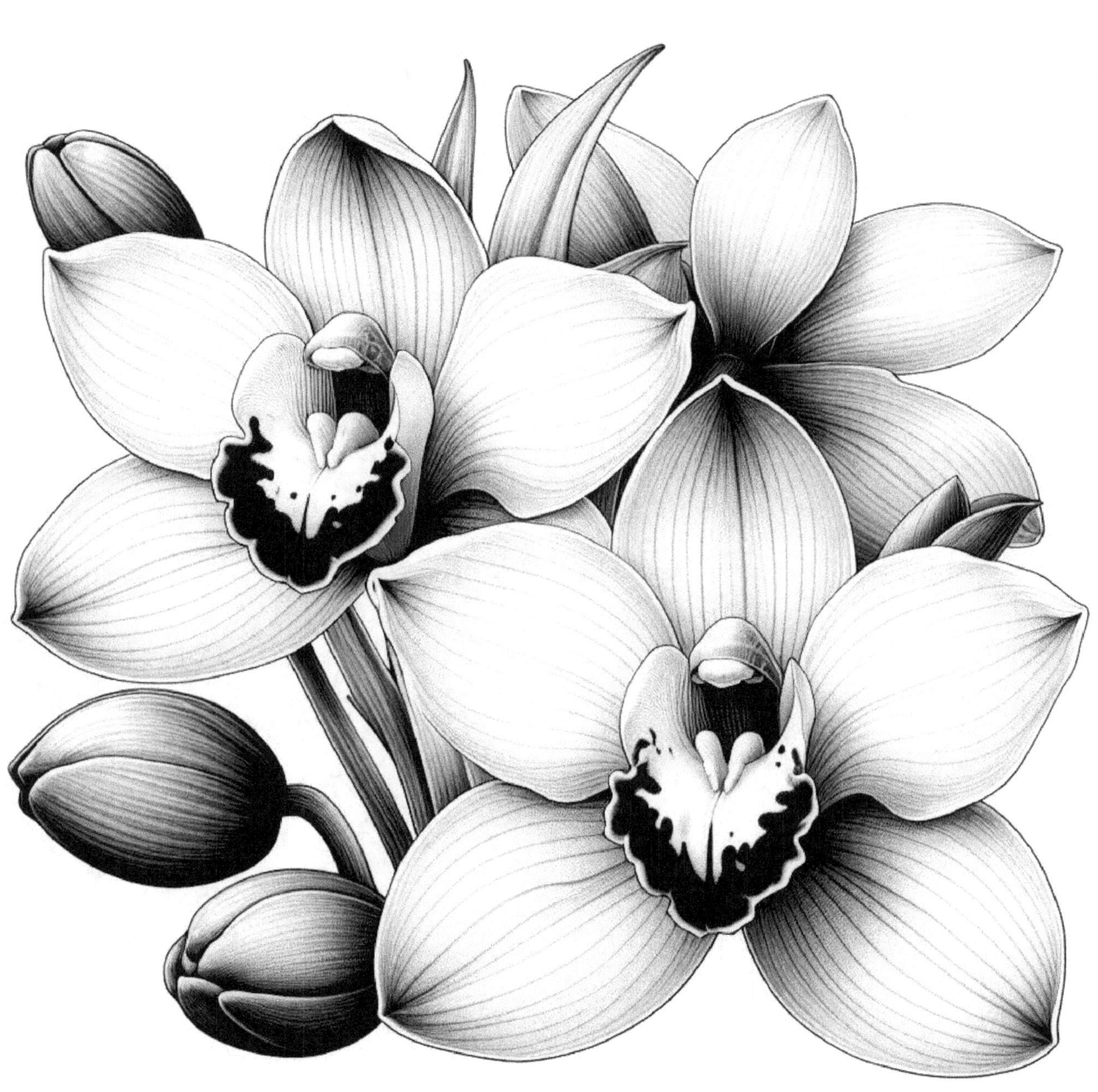

COELOGYNE

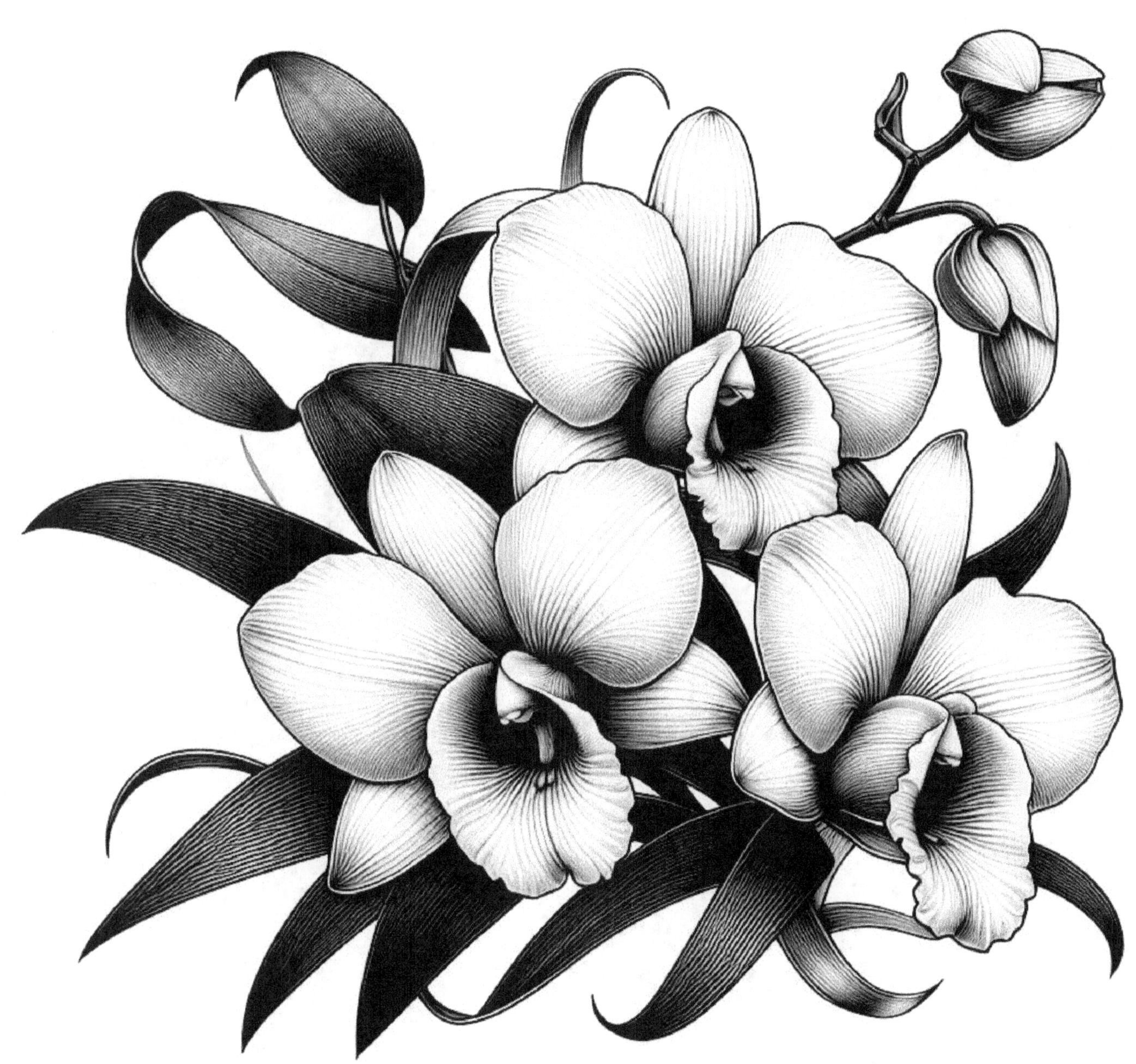

COELOGYNE

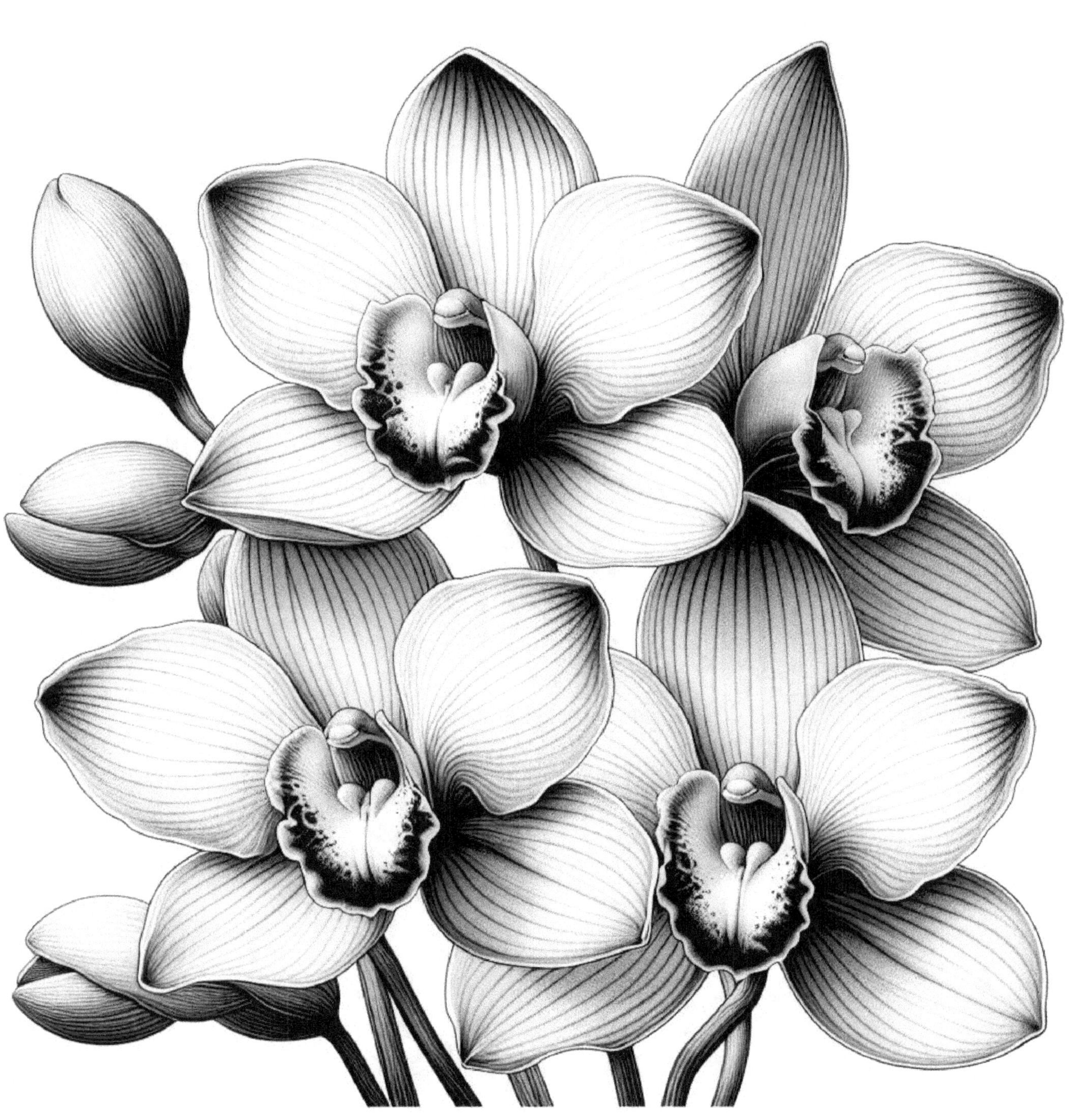

VANDA

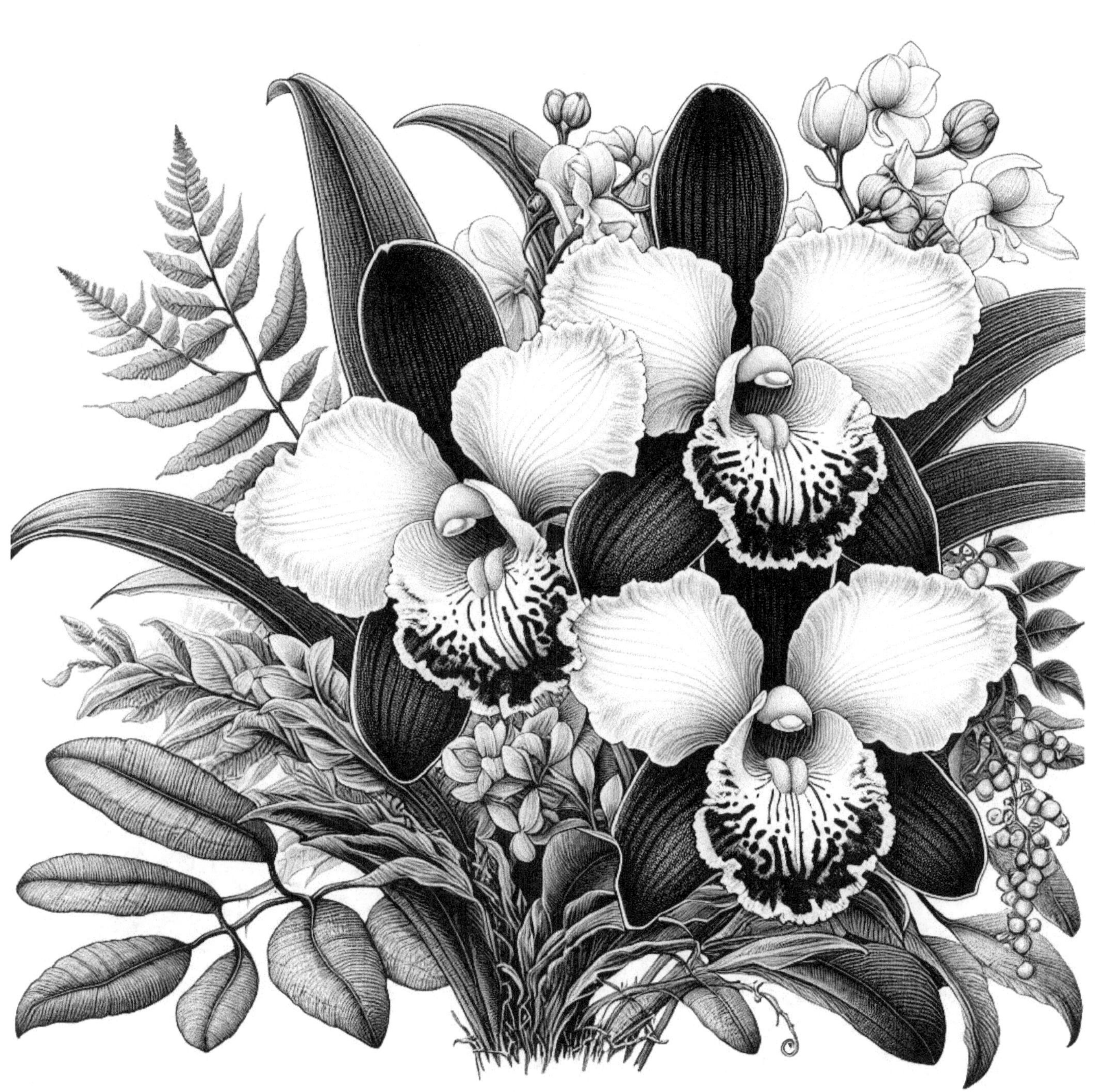

VANDA

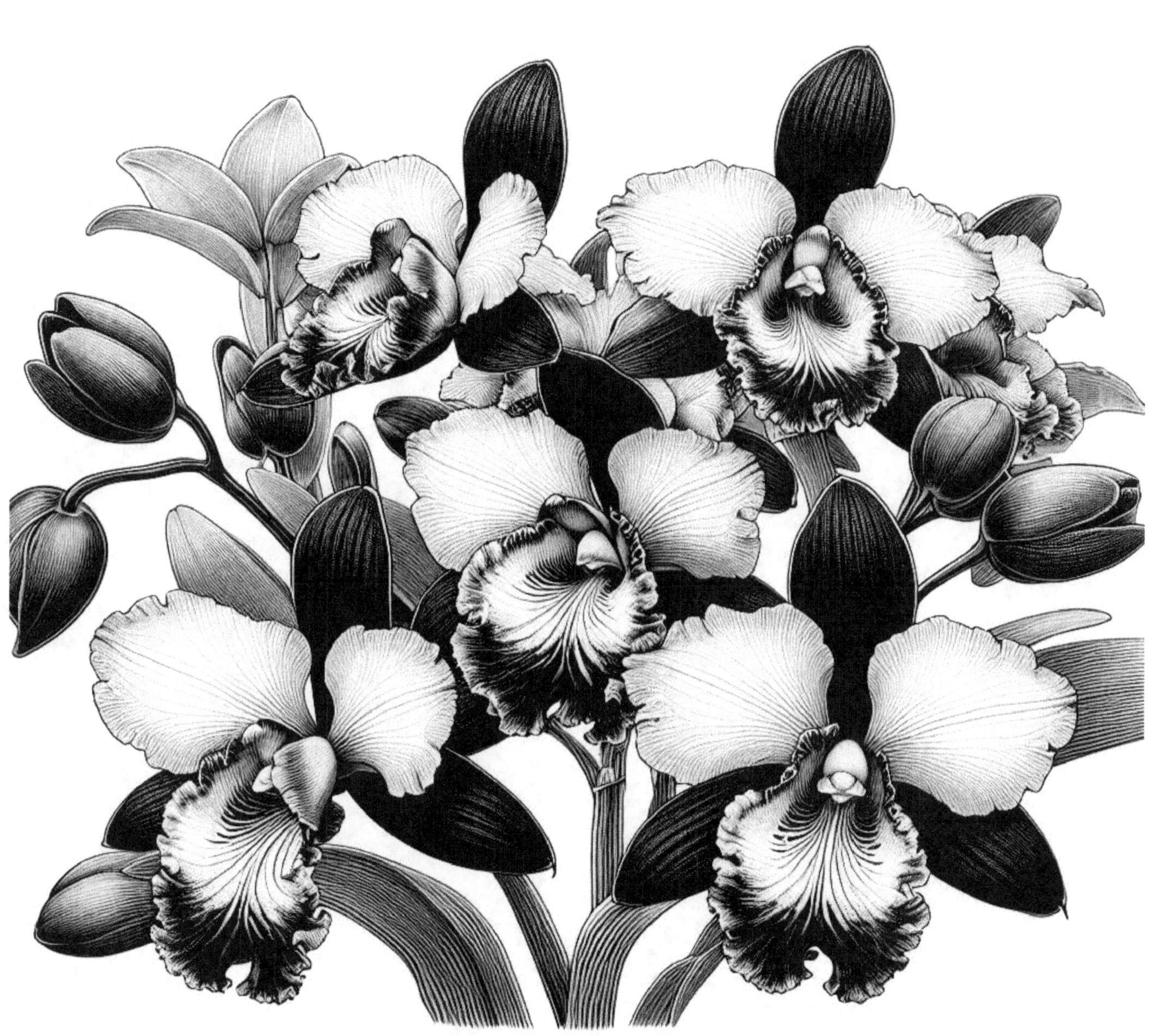

VANDA

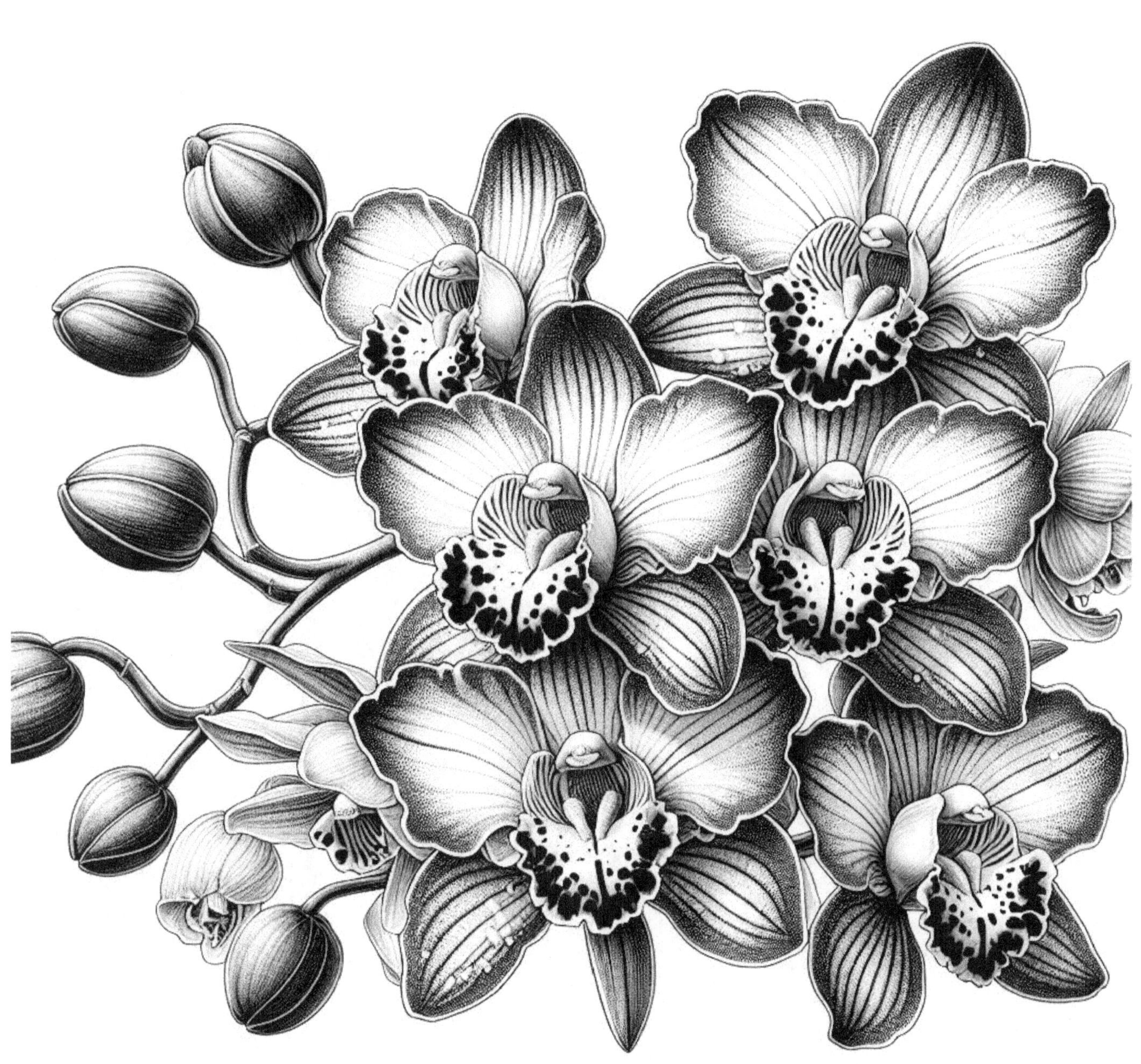

VANDA

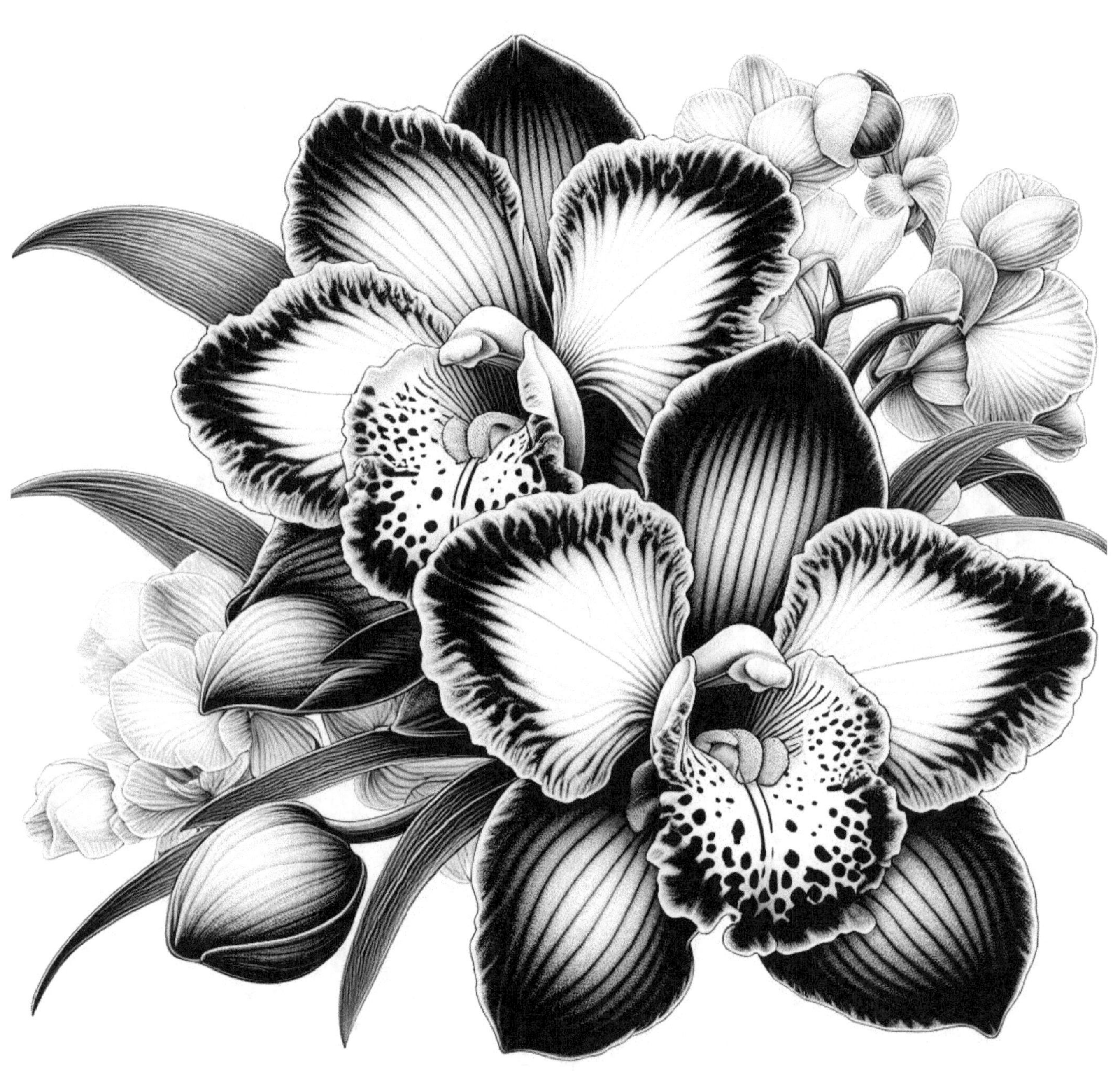

ONCIDIUM

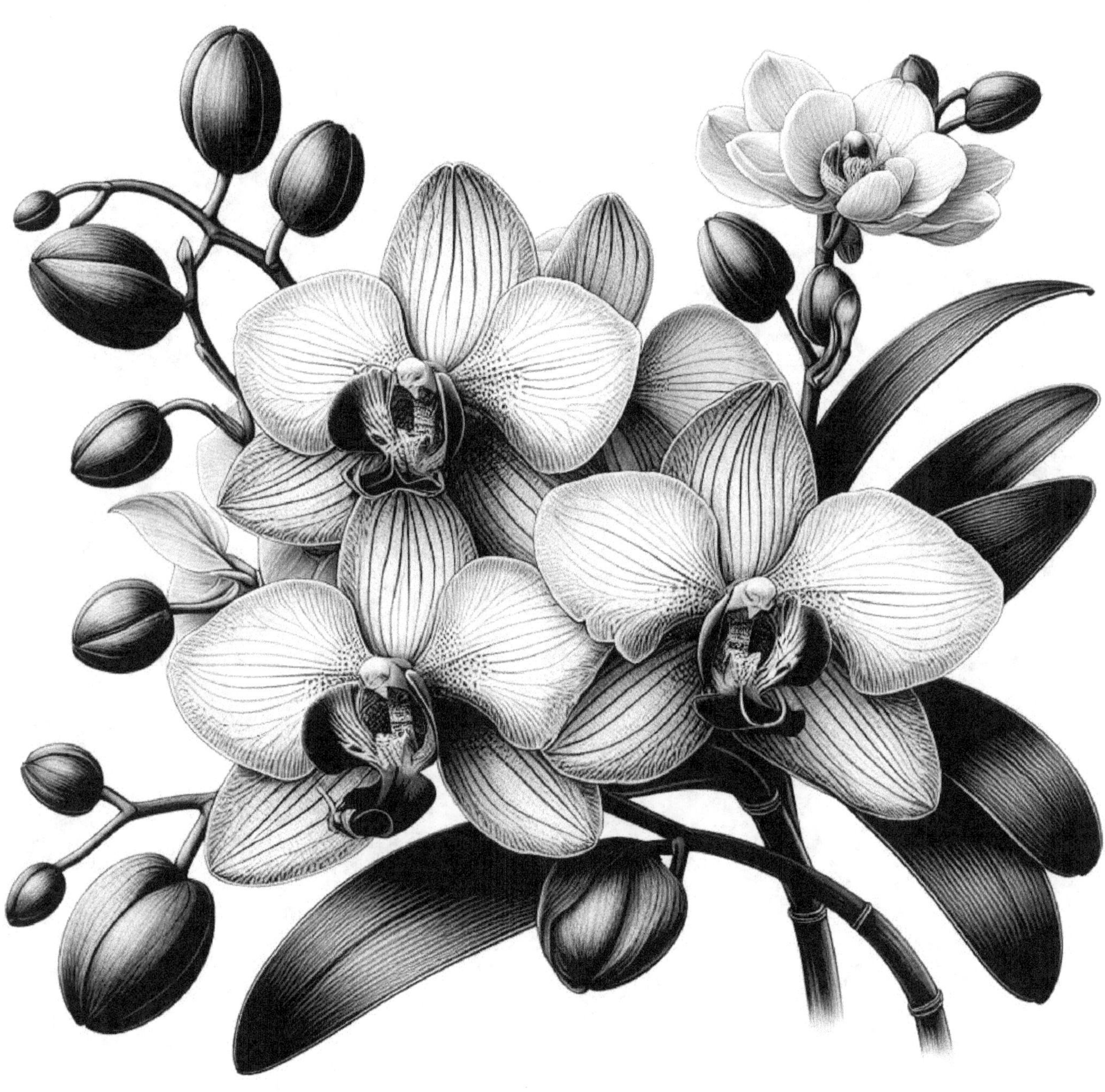

ONCIDIUM

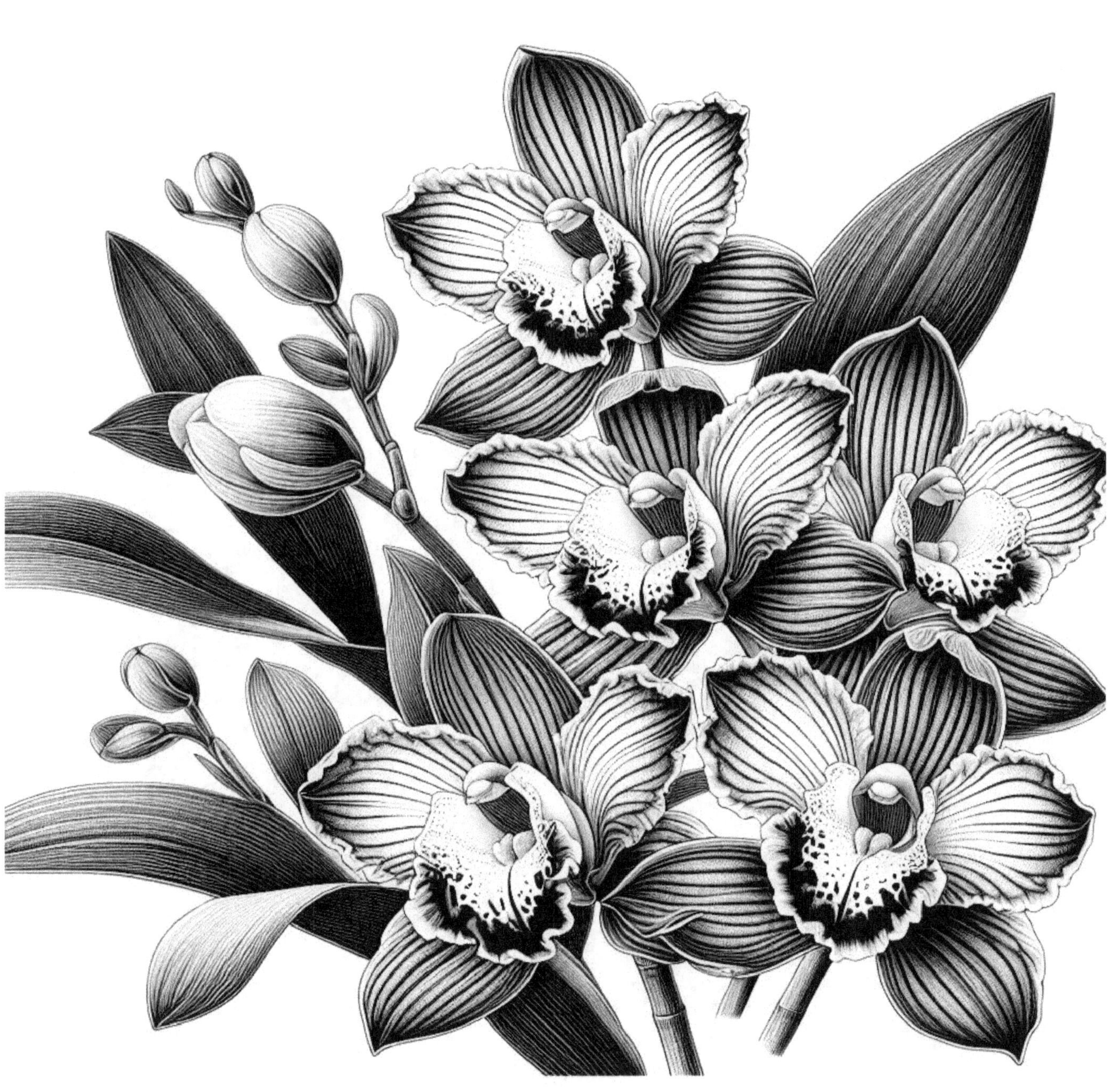

ONCIDIUM

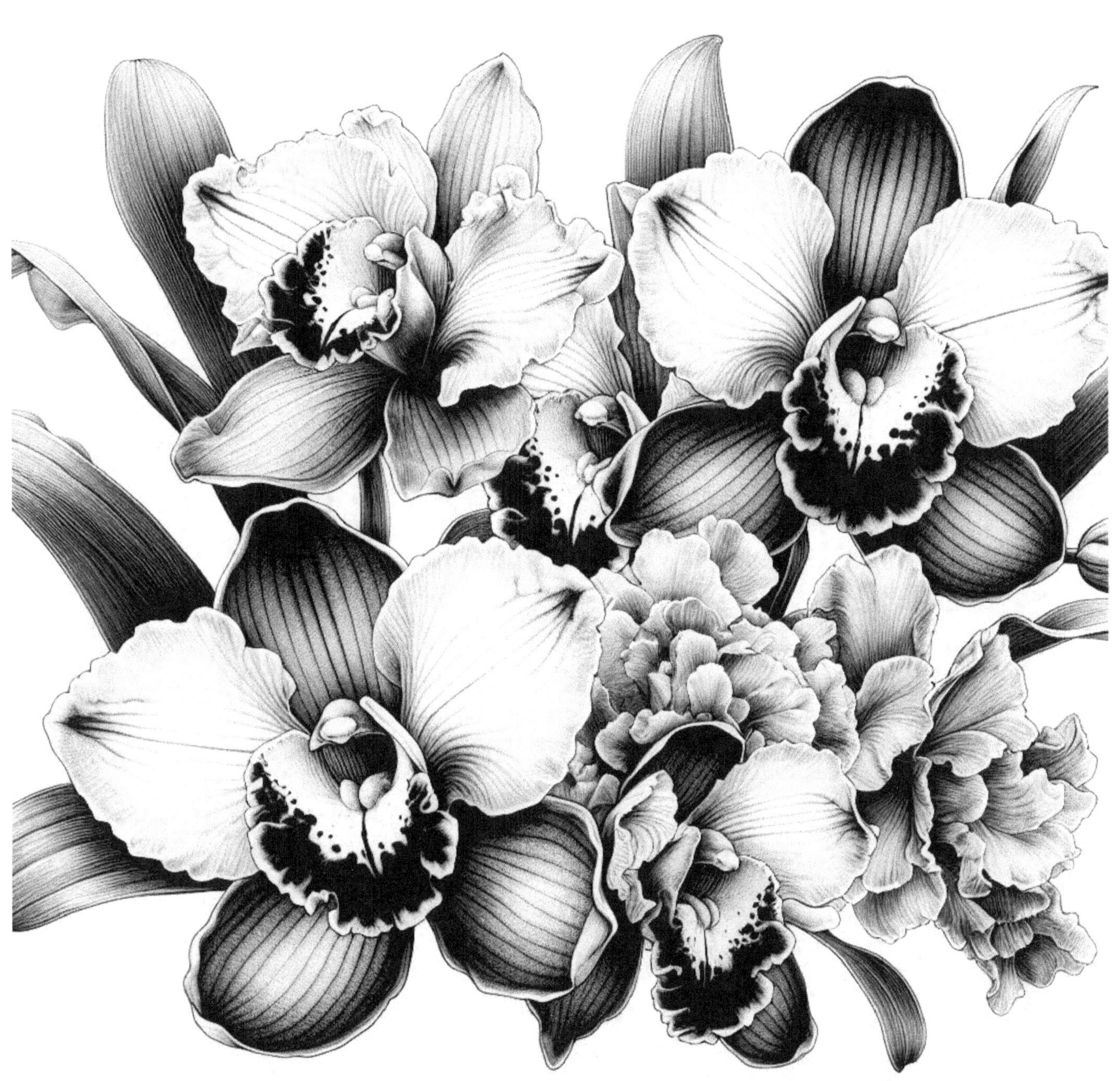

ONCIDIUM

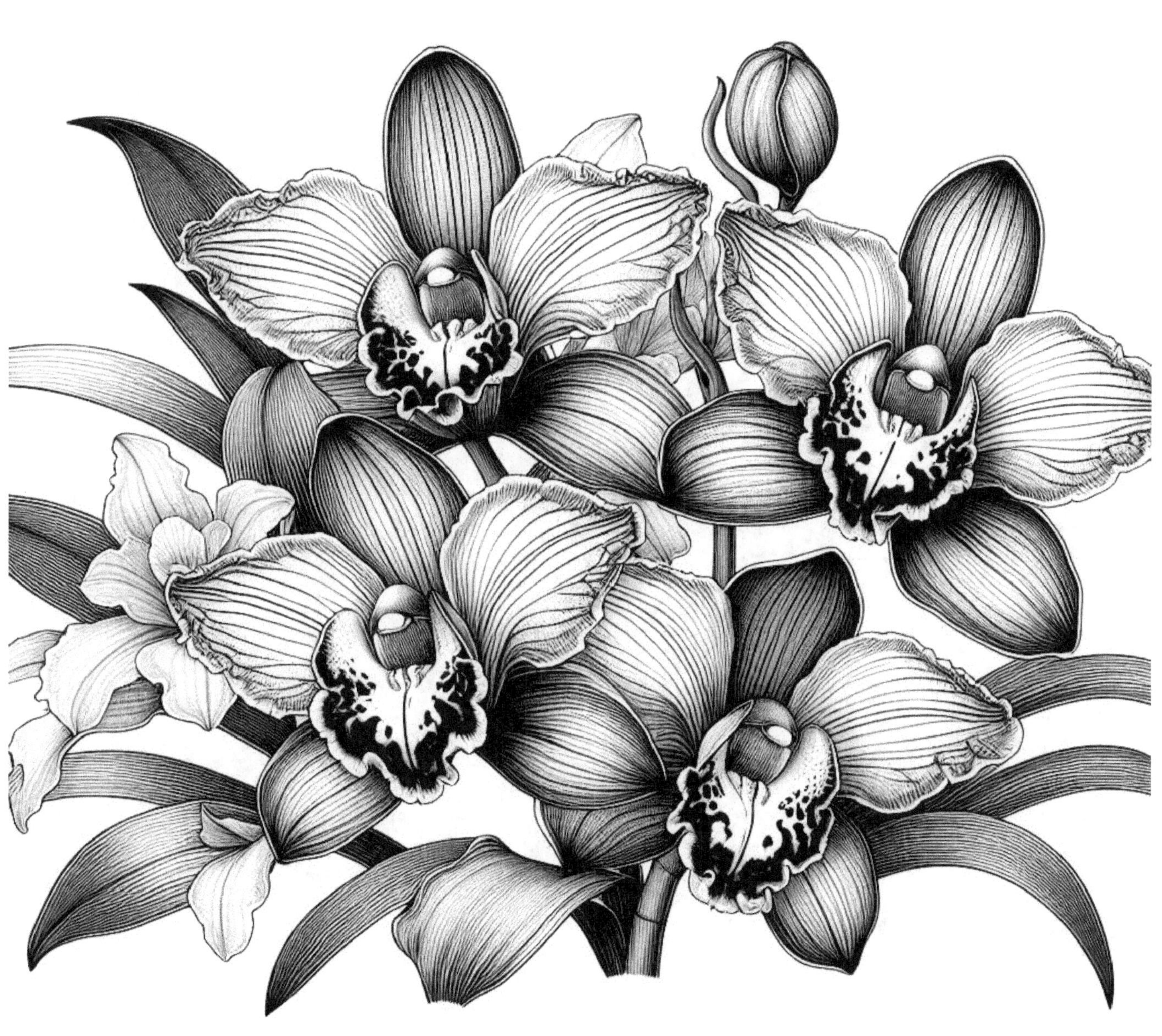

LYCASTE

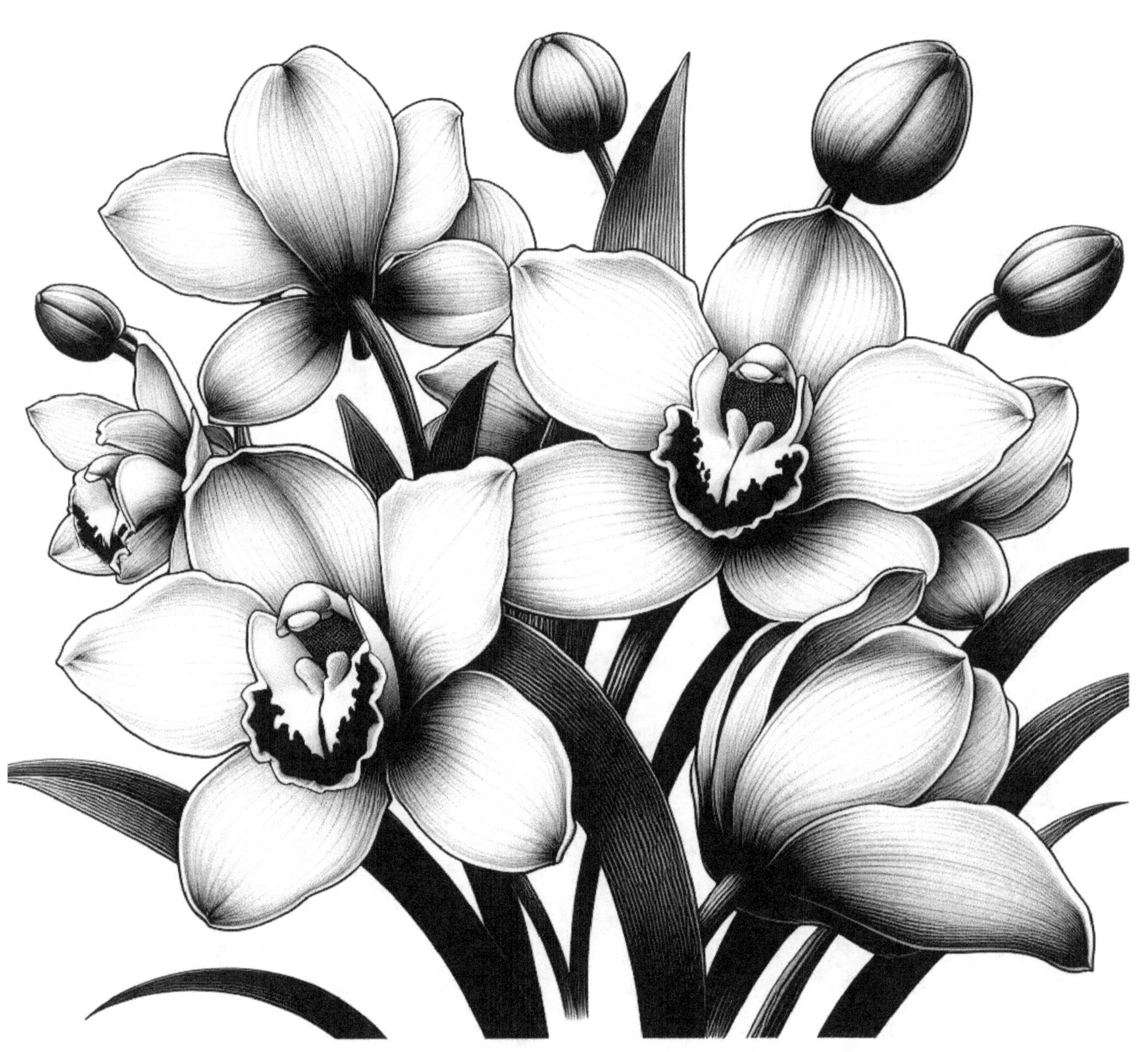

LYCASTE

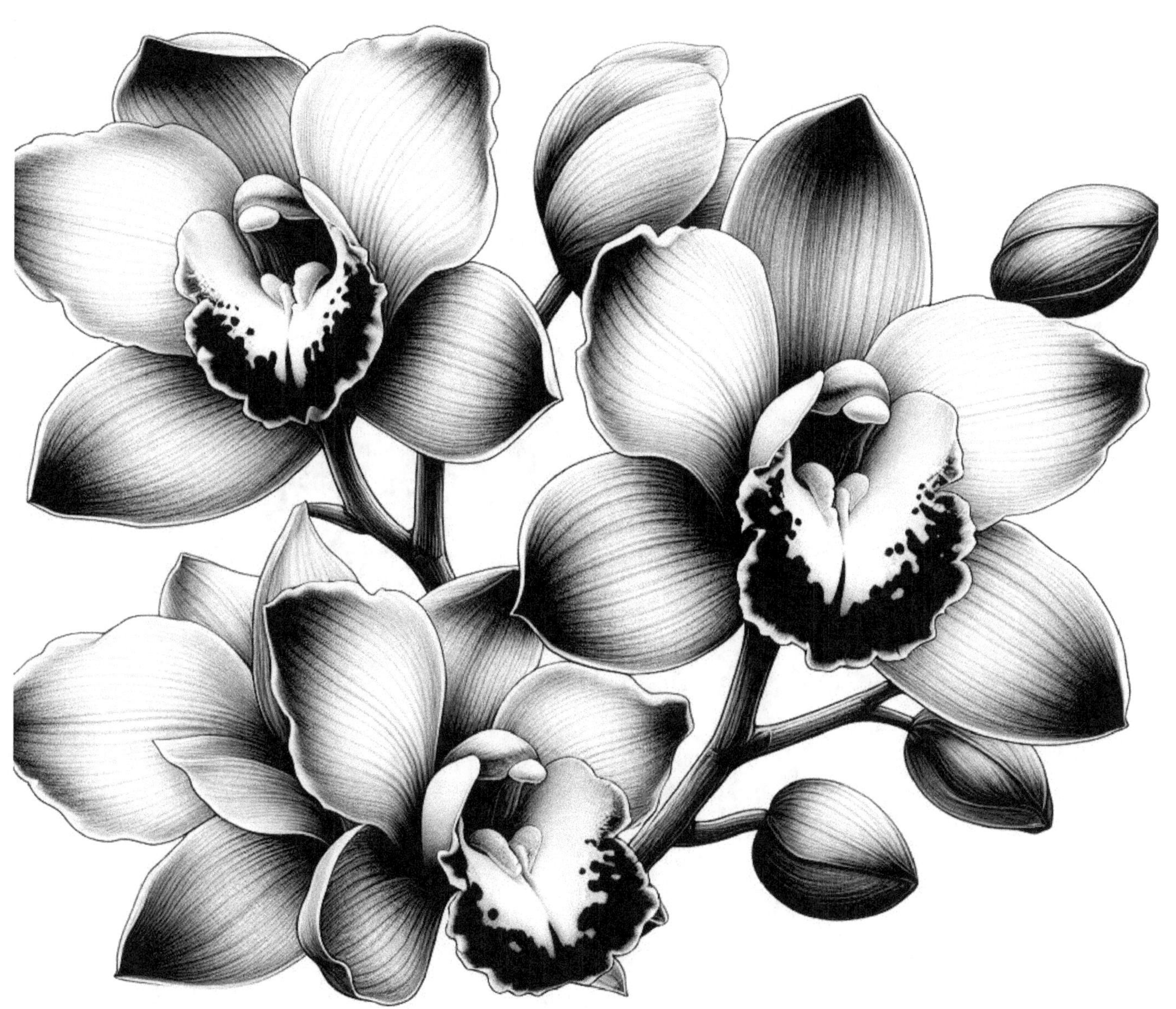

LYCASTE

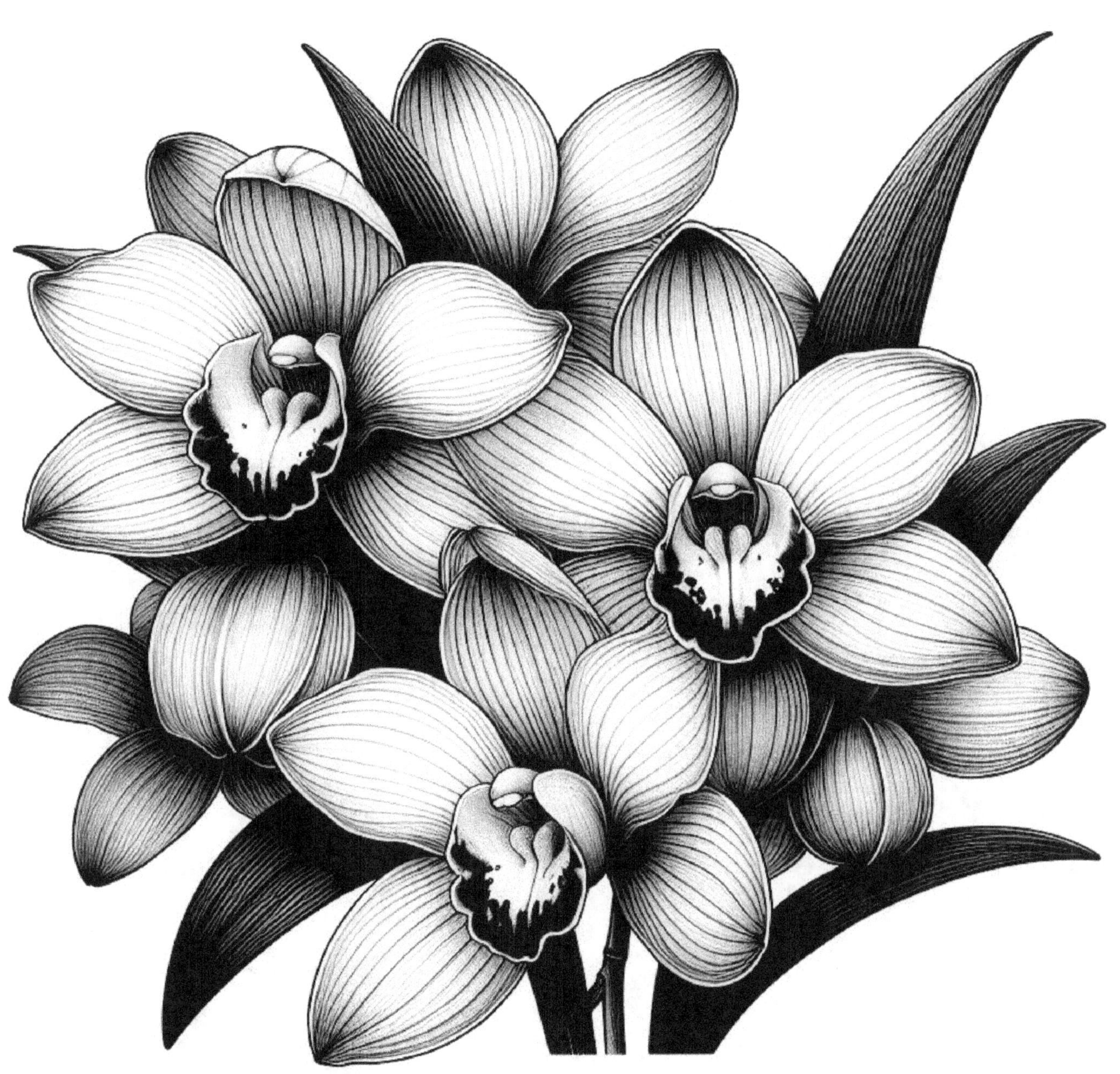

LYCASTE

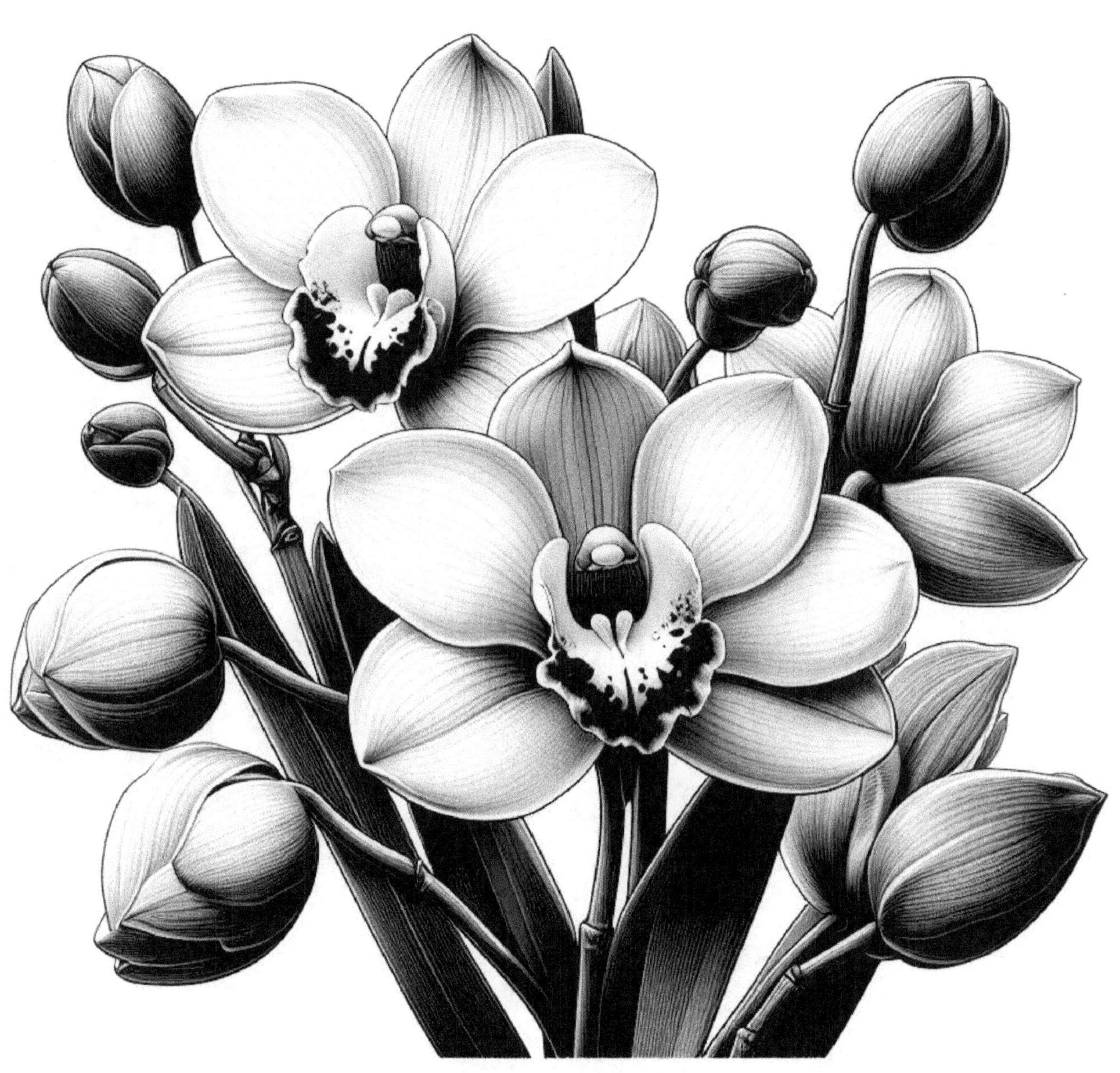

CAMBRIA

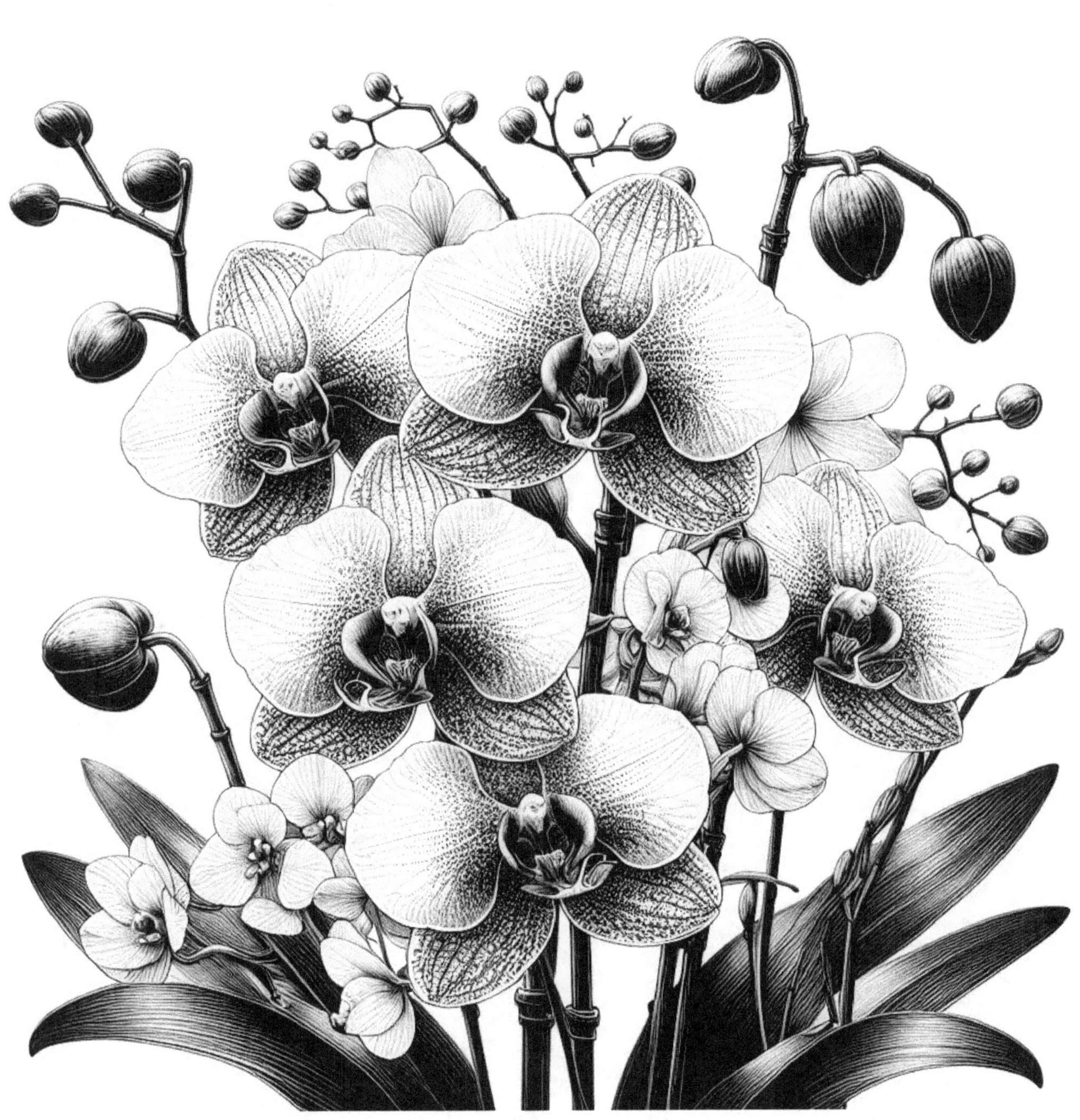

CAMBRIA

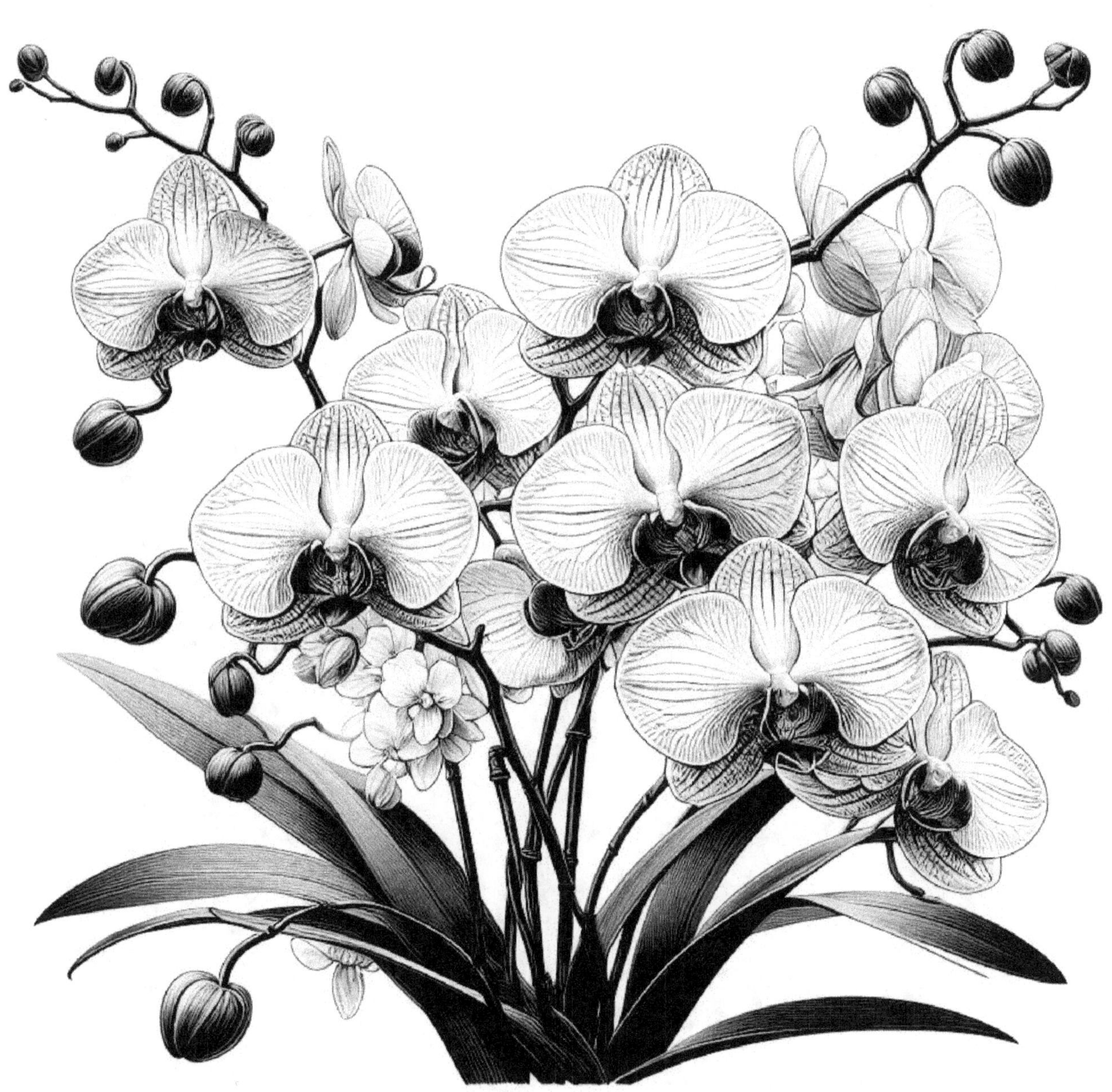

CAMBRIA

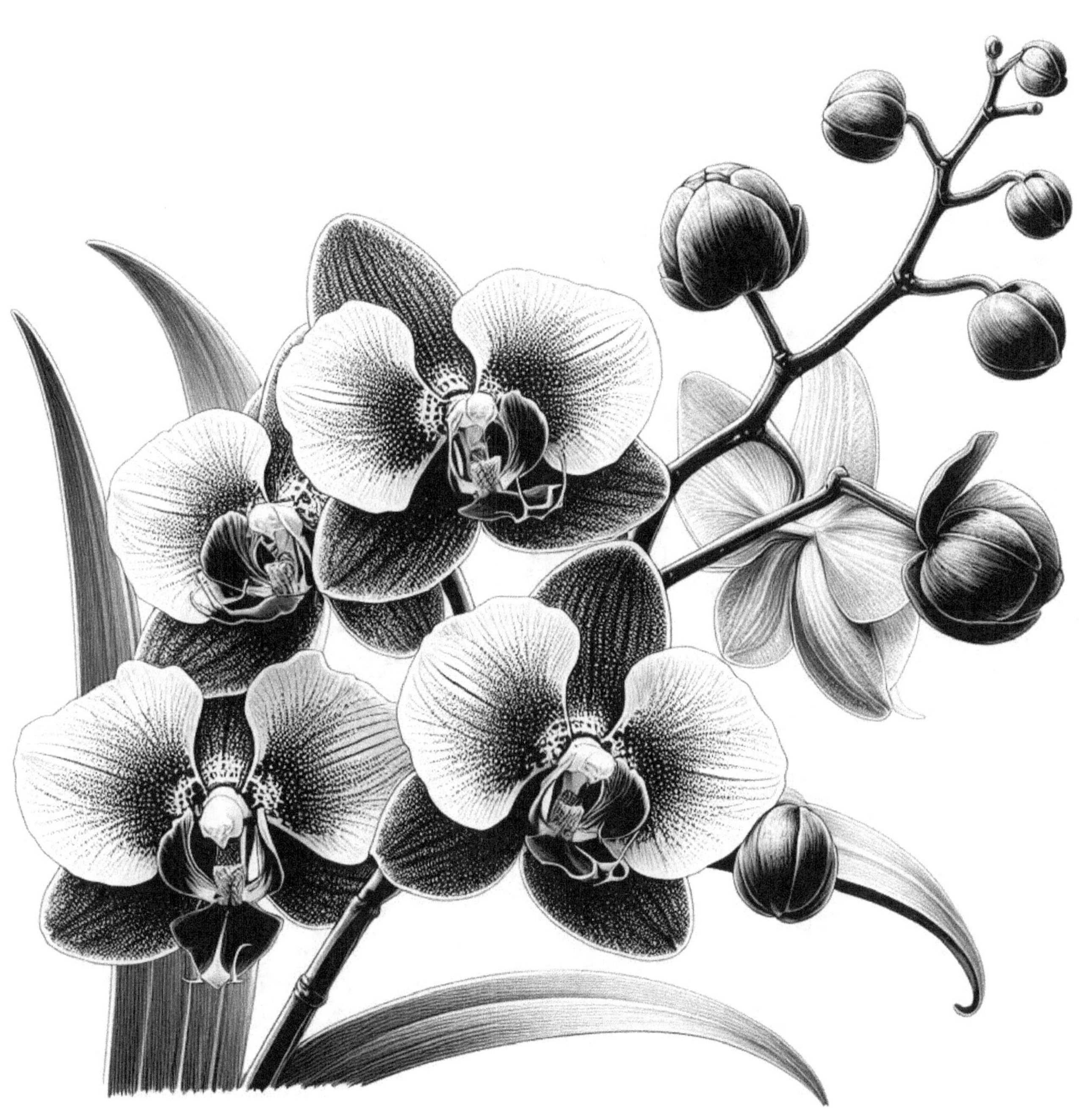

CAMBRIA

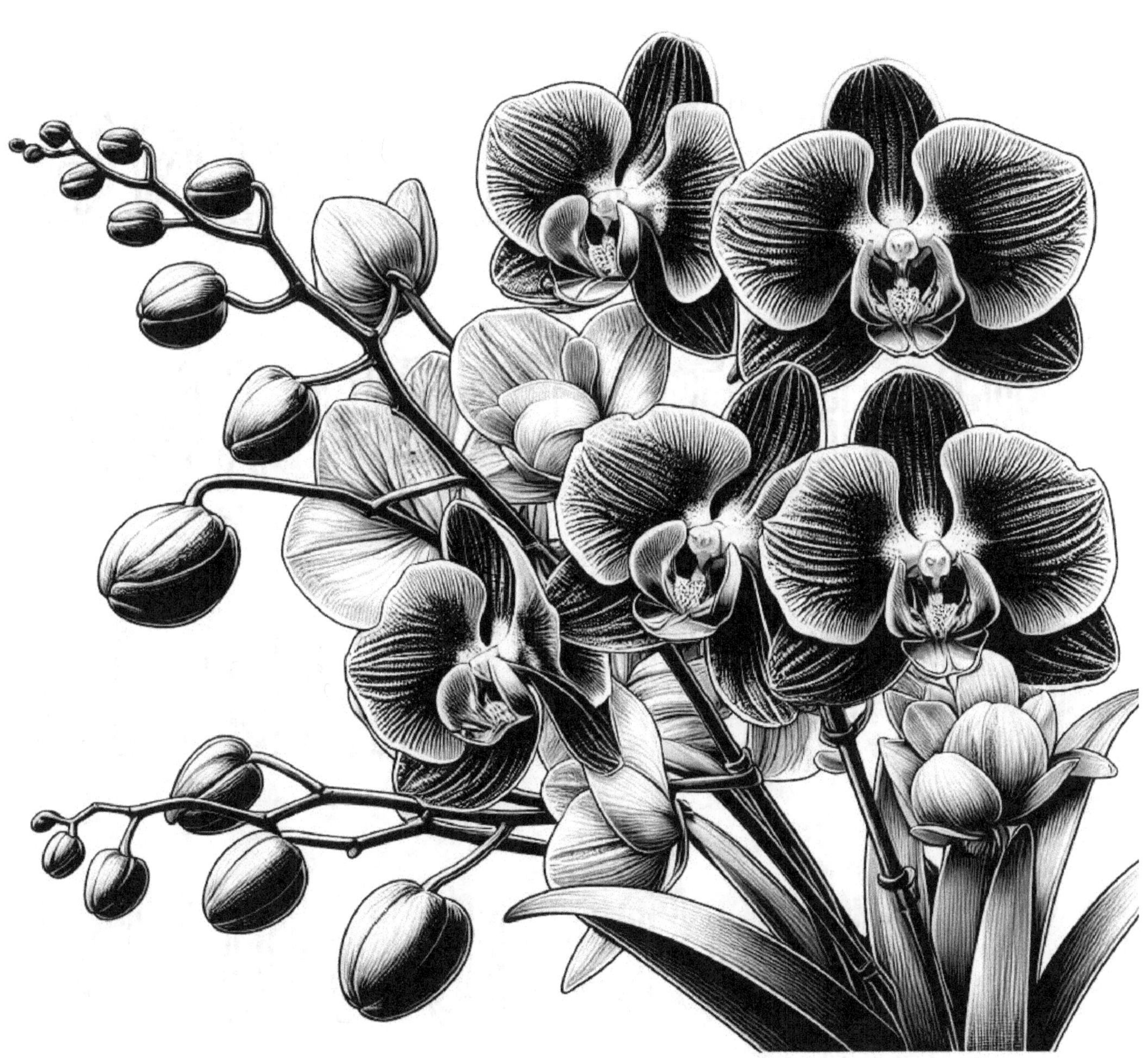

USE THE FOLLOWING PAGES TO DRAW AND TRACE THE ORCHIDS IN YOUR SURROUNDINS!